MAGNETIC
CHRISTIANITY

Gus Lloyd
P.O. Box 340983
Tampa, FL 33694-0983
http://GusLloyd.com

Cover design and layout by Nick France
http://nick**france**design.com

ISBN 978-0-615-58700-4

Printed in the USA

MAGNETIC CHRISTIANITY

USING YOUR GOD-GIVEN GIFTS TO BUILD THE KINGDOM

GUS LLOYD

ACKNOWLEDGMENTS

A project like writing a book is much like giving birth. Though I have never actually given birth, I have been intimately involved in the process. There is a lot of prayer, hard work, sweat and hand wringing involved. In the end, all you can do is put it in God's hands.

I start by thanking my bride, Michelle. After thirty-one plus years of marriage, we are still madly in love. Thank you for your patience and insights. I think we make a great team!

It is always great to work with talented people, and Nick France is among the most talented I have had the pleasure of working with. Nick, your keen eye, knowledge and love of the Lord has made for another fun journey.

When we have the chance to work with dear friends, it hardly seems like work at all. Jim Neal, one of my dearest friends, is a pro's pro in the industry. He has shepherded me through the process of bringing a book to life for the second time. Jim, I am so proud to call you my friend. Next lunch is on me!

Thanks to my mom, Barbara Egts, and to two dear friends, Julie Musselman and Becky Zentmeyer, for their wisdom and expertise in helping to edit the book. I am honored to call you friends.

I am grateful to all the listeners of my radio show, Seize the Day on Sirius XM. I learn so much from being a part of such a great community each day.

Finally, to my children, Emily, Carly, Patrick and John. I hope that my fatherhood in some miniscule way mirrors that of your true Father. It's cool that you all turned out so magnetic!

To Michelle,

the most Magnetic Christian I know.

Thank you for showing me the way to heaven every day.

CONTENTS

INTRODUCTION

Living out one's faith is not an easy thing to do. I want to start this book by freely admitting that I am not always very good about sticking to the principles I will talk about here. Like everyone, I have my share of foibles and follies. In fact, I probably have my share, your share and the shares of the bulk of the population of a large nation. But I take encouragement in my shortcomings, knowing that God still has plenty of work to do with me. If there is one thing I do well, it is keeping God busy!

For the past 25 years, I have been a Catholic evangelist. Now, to some, that may seem an oxymoron. Wait a minute, they'll say. There's no such thing as a Catholic evangelist. I remember a recent encounter I had with a woman in an airport. I was reading some Henri Nouwen on my Kindle. She was sitting next to me, flipping the pages of a bulky book. She looked over and asked me if I missed the feel of turning pages. (The answer is sometimes yes, sometimes no.) We struck up a conversation and she asked me what I do for a living. I told her I am a radio host and Catholic evangelist. At first she looked at me like I had three eyes. She crinkled her nose and said, "I didn't know there was such a thing." As God would have it, she was a wonderful Christian woman, very devoted to the Lord. We wound up having a very Spirit-filled conversation. She told me about some Catholic friends she has always admired and who had worked closely with her family in the pro-life movement. I told her they were Catholic evangelists, too!

Here is a brief synopsis of my faith story: I was raised Catholic, fell away from any faith in my late teens, then gave my life to Christ in my mid-to-late twenties. My wife, Michelle, and I began to worship at a non-denominational church. I read the Bible voraciously and grew strong in my faith. Then Michelle and I decided to look into the Catholic Church, which is where we both grew up. We rediscovered our Catholic faith and have been practicing since.

The reason I share this is to let you know that I have been on both sides of what some see as a great divide. It is part of my mission in life to help bridge this divide. While I am Catholic, many of my dearest friends are Protestant. For most people, this is no big deal. But there is a segment of the Christian population out there that does not believe that Catholics are Christian. While I understand that many of these people are well intentioned, they are dead wrong. Catholics are Christians!

Are there theological differences? Yes. There are arguments for and against each. In this book, I want nothing to do with the differences. Rather, I want to reflect on something that we hold dearly in common: the need to transform the culture. More and more people are walking away from any relationship with God. Watching Christians bicker with one another is something that I believe helps push people away. How will people see Christ in us when we can't even seem to see Christ in one another? My prayer is that, wherever you worship, you will be able to grow in faith and grace and help bring others to know the One that has changed your life and will change theirs forever.

Believe it or not, all Christians are evangelists. At least, we're supposed to be. We are called to fulfill the Great Commission given by Jesus in Matthew 28:19-20. "Go, therefore, and make disciples of all nations, baptizing them in the name of the Father, and of the Son, and of the Holy Spirit, teaching them to observe all that I have commanded you. And behold, I am with you always, until the end of the age."

Here's Big Mistake #1 that too many Christians make: they think that Jesus' command to make disciples (evangelize) is reserved only for priests and pastors and deacons and brothers and sisters and bishops and the pope and people who work for the Church. WRONG! While the clergy and religious have a special role to play in the Church and in the world, there are countless souls who may never even be exposed to one. Others may even look on them with indifference at best, and disdain at worst.

No, the real work of building up the Kingdom of God begins with me and you.

Now, I don't mean to scare you off, but I must let you know that the world is watching us. This is happening whether we like it or not, whether we accept the responsibility or not. How many times have you heard a sports star say, "I don't want to be a role model." Well, whether they want to or not, they are. Kids listen to what they say, watch what they do and want to imitate them.

The same is true of you when you profess to be a Christian. You may not stand on street corners and shout about your religion. You may not quote the Bible or even feel comfortable praying in public, aside from church on Sunday. You may not even mention your faith to anyone. But people know. At least, they should know. By the way you speak and the way you conduct yourself, your words and actions should give you away.

Well, that's all fine and good, you say. But I'm no evangelist. I'm not going to push my religion on anyone. Leave that stuff up to the Jehovah's Witnesses and Mormons. Let the Bible-thumping televangelists tell others how to live their life. I've got enough to worry about with just me.

This brings us to Big Mistake #2: To evangelize means to push your beliefs on someone else. WRONG! Evangelization has nothing to do with shoving your religion down someone else's throat or telling anyone else how to live.

At its core, I believe evangelization is simply telling others your story. Sharing the story of how God has worked and continues to work in your life. Just sharing your experiences, your journey. That's it. No preaching necessary! I know that is awfully good news to most everyone. Because while very few people like to be preached at, even fewer like to preach.

So let's start out by acknowledging that evangelization is a good thing. It is done best without being preachy, without trying to foist your beliefs on someone else. Evangelization is simply sharing the blessings that you have received. So how does one go about this evangelization process? That's what I hope you'll learn more about as you read through this book.

How To Use This Book

The beautiful thing about being human is that while we're all part of the same family, we're all quite different. God has created you as a unique, one-of-a-kind masterpiece creation of His. There has never been another human being on planet Earth that was exactly like you, and there will never ever be another person exactly like you. You have been given a distinct personality, and a very special set of gifts that only you have, and only you can use to benefit the Kingdom of God in the way that God has designed. I hope that makes you feel special, because you are!

Not only does God love you, but God wants you to use the special gifts and personality traits that you have to help others get to know you, and by getting to know you, to know God. As Christians, we have a great responsibility. We are responsible for using the gifts and talents that we have been given. We'll discuss this in much more detail later.

As we begin this journey of examining and putting into practice the things that we'll discuss, I realize that everyone has a distinctive personality. Some of the traits that we'll look at are already a strong part of who you are. Some of them may not be. Some you will be able to relate to, and others may make you feel quite uncomfortable. But that's okay. None of these traits are "better" than the others. Just because you or I may possess more of one trait or another doesn't make us better or worse than anyone else.

The purpose of this book is to help us understand how to use those traits that God has given us to draw others to Christ, and to see if there are ways we can strengthen other traits that we may be underutilizing or are even afraid of. After each chapter, do an assessment of yourself and see if you may be strong or weak in that particular attribute. Ask God if this is something He wants you to improve upon. I'm pretty sure we can all use some degree of improvement in every area. If you find that you have been blessed with an abundance of a particular attribute, praise God! Use your strengths for God's glory.

If you find that you may be weak in certain areas, praise God! These are things that you can allow God to work on. Ask God to give you opportunities and put you into situations where you can work on those things, and allow Him to fill you with whatever you need.

You may choose to read this book from cover to cover in one shot. That's fine and good. But if you do that, I suggest that, after you've finished, you go back and read it again, one chapter at a time. Spend a good bit of time with each chapter. Think of stories from your own life that may fit into the chapter. I hope you'll find that God speaks to you through it all.

I'm excited about the journey we're about to take! Are you ready? Then let's get started!

MAGNETIC CHRISTIANITY

MAJOR ATTRIBUTES OF
A MAGNETIC PERSONALITY

Have you ever met someone that drew you to them the first time you met? I think we've all met someone who, when they enter a room, all eyes are drawn to them. People gravitate towards them; they want to be near them. We've often heard this termed "personal magnetism," or think of that person as having a "magnetic personality." But have you ever really thought of what it is that makes a magnetic personality?

Let's start by eliminating a few things that some may mistakenly put on the list. At the top of the list of what doesn't constitute a magnetic personality is good looks. Now, I don't know about you, but I've met some people in my day who were very physically attractive but who no one wanted to be around. Sometimes physical attractiveness can actually be a deterrent to having a magnetic personality. Why? Because sometimes very attractive people can tend to look down their noses at others they may not deem as "hot." Madison Avenue and the world today want you to think that if you don't have a rock hard body and the face of a supermodel, you are somehow inferior. This, my friend, is a lie straight from the lips of Satan. A magnetic personality has nothing to do with how you look. This isn't to say that very attractive people can't have a magnetic personality; many certainly do. But it is not a prerequisite.

The next thing on the list is intellectualism. As with physical attractiveness, having great knowledge can also be a stumbling block to having a magnetic personality. Again, this is a sweeping generality, but I have found that some people who are uber-smart know that not only are they uber-smart, but you are not. Possessing a great deal of book smarts can be a very good thing. We should always be learning and growing in knowledge. But uber-smartness is not necessary for having a magnetic personality.

> **MAGNETIC INSIGHT:** *If we truly want to help others, then it is our duty to help them understand that a relationship with God is the one thing – the only thing – that will give them true joy.*

Next up – money! When you first meet someone with a magnetic personality, you probably don't know how much money they have. Hopefully you don't care. There are plenty of people with boatloads of cash I wouldn't let my dog go near. As well, there are plenty of people who don't have two nickels to rub together that you just can't get enough of. Some people may be attracted to money, but money cannot buy attractiveness. You may be able to buy a nose job or a face lift or liposuction, but you can't buy the things that make a magnetic personality.

The last two things on our list of things that DON'T make for a magnetic personality are power and fame. Isn't it interesting that these are two things many people would sell their soul for? Yet, just like all the other things on this list, power and fame have nothing to do with having a magnetic personality. Some people may achieve power or fame because of their magnetic personalities, but it does not happen in the opposite order.

That's a short list and I'm sure we could come up with many others. I want you to notice the things on the list are things so many people today are striving after. They've bought the bill of goods that being "hot" or smart or rich or powerful or famous is going to fulfill them. But you and I both know that this is a false gospel. Life is really all about relationships. We can only find true happiness, peace and joy by enhancing our relationship with God, and our relationships with others.

If we truly want to help others (and I hope that we do), then it is our duty to help them understand that a relationship with God is the one thing – the only thing – that will give them true joy. Because as we all develop that deeper relationship with God, it will only enhance our relationships with others. But first people must be drawn to God. That's where you and your Magnetic Christianity come in!

Ever since I was a young man, I have been a fan of the "self-help" genre of books. I am a big believer in the power of the mind. Books by people like Norman Vincent Peale, Napoleon Hill, Zig Ziglar and Dale Carnegie have had a profound influence on me. I believe their basic principles are right on the money.

I have always had something of a problem with some of the ideas presented in some circles of "self-help" thinking. Where does God fit into all of this? And can we find these principles in God's word? The answer, of course, is yes! There have been and continue to be many great books written by brilliant Christian authors that will help you to be happier and more successful. But I want you to know those are not the end goals of this book. Don't get me wrong; if you allow God to strengthen you in the attributes we talk about in this book, you may, indeed, become happier and more successful. And that's great! But the bottom line is that this book is not, in the end, about you. It is not about what you can get from enhancing your relationship with God and utilizing your gifts to the full. It is about what you can give. It is about fulfilling your potential so you can help others to find the ultimate happiness: life in Christ.

The term "self-help" is troublesome to begin with. It implies that the help we need to succeed as humans lies within ourselves, or we can tap into this on our own power. For some, this seems like a rather atheistic viewpoint. It makes it seem as though we

> **MAGNETIC INSIGHT:**
> *So many people will never encounter Christ unless they encounter Him in us.*

are the be-all and the end-all; as though the power that lies within us comes from us.

As a Christian, we must reject this notion. Any power that we have comes from God alone. The moment we begin to take credit for anything is the moment we begin to fall into the sin of pride. I want to state from the outset that this is THE underlying principle of this book. We all have great power within us. But that power does not come FROM us. The traits and attributes we will cover are all gifts from Almighty God. We must always recognize this, acknowledge it and be sure to give thanks for all the gifts that have been given to us.

That being said, we have all been given great power. The human mind is one of the most complex and powerful things ever created by God. This would only stand to reason if we believe that we have been created in the image and likeness of God. (Genesis 2) This does not mean that we are God or gods. I'm afraid too many people make this mistake. It's the whole pride thing. But we are "God-like" in that we resemble God; we are His children, His offspring. He has endowed us with power that is beyond our wildest dreams, even our own comprehension. The power God has given us is the power to tap into His power!

Now to him who is able to accomplish far more than all we ask or imagine, by the power at work within us, to him be glory in the church and in Christ Jesus to all generations, forever and ever. Amen.
Ephesians 3:20-21

We speak of the power of our minds. But we must always be cautious in using this power. If left to our own devices, we will invariably misuse this awesome power. We must always be sure that our mind is working in tandem with our heart. By this I mean the laws God has written onto our hearts. We must always be striving to be within God's will. The one place we can be sure we find this is in the sacred Scriptures.

Does God's word speak of a magnetic personality? It certainly does! In fact, the Lord Jesus had the most magnetic personality of all time! If we can just imitate Christ, others will naturally be drawn to us. But the goal is not to draw people to us as though we're collecting sycophants. The goal is to draw people to us so they can see Christ working through us. The real goal is to draw people to Christ! We must remember that we are the hands and feet of Jesus. So many people will never encounter Christ unless they encounter Him in us. So let's move forward and reflect on the attributes we can better utilize to help draw others to Christ.

The following list is certainly not exhaustive. In fact, I'm sure you can come up with other things that you feel make up a Magnetic Personality. That's great! Write them down and add them to the list! I've identified eleven things I find clear evidence for in the Scriptures that I believe will draw others to us, and to Christ, like a magnet attracts metal. Hone in on these eleven attributes. Work on growing in each area. They will serve you well in every area of your life – family, business relationships, friendships, ministry – you name it!

Here are the eleven attributes of a Magnetic Personality:

- Positivity

- Enthusiasm

- Friendliness

- Confidence

- Humility

- Honesty

- Kindness

- Compassion

- Approachability

- Generosity

- Encouragement

Each chapter will be filled with Scripture references that speak to the attribute at hand. Meditate on these passages. See if you can think of others that relate to the attribute. Seek out deeper answers in God's word. I'm sure that, as you discover other verses, you'll have one "Aha!" moment after another. At the end of each chapter, I'll give you some questions to use as thought starters or discussion starters. As you reflect on them, try to bring up situations from your past where you found success in using the attribute. Realize each success was a gift to you from the Holy Spirit. Think, too, of times where you may have fallen short, where you may not have utilized the attribute as well as you could have. These are moments we can certainly learn from. It's often said that we learn more from our failures than from our successes. I believe we can learn much from both, especially in the spiritual life.

So, what are we waiting for? Come on! Let's grow!

CHAPTER ONE

POSITIVITY

Rejoice in the Lord always. I shall say it again: rejoice!
Philippians 4:4

I t's probably the most common question in the English language. It can also be one of the trickiest. The answer to the question can reveal an awful lot about a person's attitude, demeanor, and outlook on life. What is the question?

"How are you?" (The question has any number of variations, like "How's it going?" and "How are you doing?" or "How ya doin'?")

How do you answer that question? I've found the most common answer is a one word answer. "Fine." And that's... well, fine. But is it true? And if so, is it enough? I hope not!

Fine simply says things could be better. On the positive side, things could be worse, too. But why should we settle for fine? When I hear someone answer "fine," it makes me think that perhaps that person's life has gotten into a rut. Is "fine" the best that life has to offer? Is "fine" all that God wants for you? I say certainly not!

Back to our answers to the question. Over the course of my life I've had a number of responses. Lately I've been stuck on two: "Fantastic!" and "Better than I deserve!" But I've heard a lot of other answers I think are very cool, too. Two of them were favorites of my dad, who passed away in October of 2008. If ever there was a guy with a magnetic personality, it was Phil Lloyd! Pop's favorite answers?

"If I were any better I'd have to be twins!" On days when he was feeling particularly frisky, he would up it to triplets. His other favorite was "Finer than frog hair!"

I have a dear friend, Barney, whose answer is always, "I'm blessed!"

Another friend, Tom Hoopes, always said, "Tremendous!" I liked that one so much I wrote a song as an intro for the segment he used to have on my radio show. I started calling him "The Tremendous One."

My friend Lino Rulli, the Catholic Guy, likes to respond, "Mint!"

Unfortunately, there are some who feel that the question is an open invitation to spill about all of the ills that have befallen them in their lives. These poor souls just ooze negativity. While they certainly need our prayers, they're probably someone you're going to avoid in the future. If nothing else, you'll come up with a different opening line when you see them, right? I mean, who wants to be bombarded with negativity? No one! And as Christians, we have nothing to be negative about. Quite the contrary. We need to be a people of rejoicing! So how can you reflect that in answering the world's most common question? Think of how your answer to that may just help to brighten up someone's day. Let's get rid of "I'm fine," and replace it with something that reflects more clearly God's goodness in our lives.

> *Shout joyfully to the LORD, all you lands;*
> *worship the LORD with cries of gladness;*
> *come before him with joyful song.*
> *Know that the LORD is God,*
> *our maker to whom we belong,*
> *whose people we are, God's well-tended flock.*
> *Enter the temple gates with praise,*
> *its courts with thanksgiving.*
> *Give thanks to God, bless his name,*
> *good indeed is the LORD,*
> *Whose love endures forever,*
> *whose faithfulness lasts through every age.*
> ***Psalm 100***

Maybe you've heard this old expression:

"If you're happy, let your face know."

As children of God, we have the most awesome, unbelievable treasure of all time! Eternal life through Jesus Christ! How can we not be positive about life? God has blessed you with the gift of life, and the gift of faith. Yet so many Christians are walking through life like expressionless zombies. While I am a big fan of zombie flicks (guilty pleasure), I daresay that I would not be attracted to a zombie should one ever cross my path. In fact, I'm pretty sure that I would run in the opposite direction as fast as my legs would carry me. So it is with people who meet up with Christian zombies. With that in mind, I offer you this piece of advice:

• DON'T BE A CHRISTIAN ZOMBIE!

Learn to smile more. Practice that wry smile that will make other people wonder what you're thinking or what you're up to. That's the one that is more likely to entice someone to ask you

> **MAGNETIC INSIGHT:**
> *God has a plan for your life, and that plan is not a small plan. God wants great things for you!*

what you're smiling about. Then...Bingo! An opportunity to share your story. See? More Smiles = More Jesus.

> *What then shall we say to this? If God is for us,*
> *who can be against us?*
> **Romans 8:31**

Saint Paul asks the question: If God is for us, who can be against us? It may seem like a rhetorical question, but I believe it has an answer. Do you know what the answer is? WHO CARES?? That's the answer to the question. If God is for us, it doesn't matter who is against us. And I can tell you most assuredly, God is for you. God only wants what is best for you at all times. Please don't make the mistake so many make and think that God wants to fulfill your every desire. That's not how God works. Why? Because God knows not all of our desires are good or holy or within His will. Because of our fallen nature, many of our desires would do nothing more than lead us away from God. What kind of loving parent would do things intentionally that they knew would push their children away? Things they knew would be harmful to their children? Our God would never do that! Because God is a loving Father, and a loving Father always wants what is best for his children.

A Plan for Your Life

Have you ever felt like the whole world is against you? I think we all feel that way at one time or another. I have struggled with depression. It's a nasty, joy-sucking malady. During a few of my nastier bouts, I truly felt alone, like the whole world was against me. But that was only in my own mind. Nothing could have been further from the truth. My wife, my family, my friends were all pulling for me. Most of them didn't even know I was suffering. Many who suffer from depression are very good at hiding it. At least, they think they are. I guess the reason for me telling you this is to let you know that even when you think the whole world is against you, you're wrong. God has put people in your life who love you and care about you deeply. Remember, God is always for you.

My friend, you have been put here for a purpose. In fact, you are holding this book in your hand for a purpose. God has a plan for your life, and that plan is not a small plan. God wants great things for you! In saying this, I feel it necessary to offer some perspective. The world's definition of "great" may differ wildly with God's definition of "great." Too often, we think in terms of the world's definition. We think that "great" means getting noticed - noticed by the world, of course. But the truly great things we will accomplish on this earth are things that are noticed by God, things the world may never see.

Let me give a quick example: Blessed Mother Teresa of Calcutta. Mother Teresa was known the world over. We all know about how she inspired millions of people and built hospitals and orphanages and founded an order of nuns who have helped countless souls. But if you asked Mother Teresa about the great things she had done, I'm certain that none of those things would have crossed her lips. She would probably tell you the greatest things she did were things like holding the hand of a person dying of malnutrition in the street. Or comforting a victim of AIDS. Or reminding someone of how much God loves them. Things that were never noticed by folks with cameras and microphones.

Yes, God has great things in store for you. Let's always remember to use God's definition of greatness. Stop comparing yourself to others. Because just like you, the plan that God has for your life is unique. Nobody else's plan is like yours, and your plan is like nobody else's.

For I know well the plans I have in mind for you, says the
LORD, plans for your welfare, not for woe!
plans to give you a future full of hope.
Jeremiah 29:11

Life Lessons

These are tough times we're living in. Too many of our neighbors are unemployed or underemployed. Real estate values and 401(k) balances continue to sink like a little kid's stomach who has been summoned to the principal's office. To many, the future looks bleak. This cannot be the attitude of the Magnetic Christian! When we allow ourselves to fall prey to the gloom-and-doomers, we chip away at our faith in God. We negate God's word! Who are you going to believe – will it be some talking head on the TV or radio or Internet telling you all is lost? Or some politician who screams that if you don't support his or her plan, your future is in jeopardy? Or will you believe God Almighty? Let's see, last time I checked, God Almighty has more credibility than any talking head or politician or anyone else who wants to tell you your future isn't as bright as a supernova! So, we'll trust God on this one.

> **MAGNETIC INSIGHT:**
> *Almighty God IS involved in the mission of your life. If you truly believe that God is with you, then you must believe that anything is possible for you.*

Now we know that our future is bright. But what about the present? What about those hard times, those situations you may be going through right now that are sapping your strength, draining your energy? How are we supposed to look at all this? Once again, St. Paul comes to the rescue!

We know that all things work for good for those who love
God, who are called according to his purpose.
Romans 8:28

Life is full of lessons. In fact, I believe that is one of the main purposes for our lives - to learn lessons. Remember, God has a purpose and a plan for your life. He has planted greatness within you. However, that doesn't mean life is going to be without trials. Jesus spoke often about how His disciples would be hated, beaten, even killed. When you think about it, it's a wonder Christianity ever got off the ground! I mean, who really wants to sign up for that kind of duty?

Jesus: "Oh, by the way, everyone will hate you, you'll be beaten up, and chances are pretty good that you'll die a painful and horrific death."

Disciple: "Hey, Teacher, look at the time! Seems I've got a...uh...dentist's appointment! Yeah, that's the ticket! I'll check back with you later."

Luckily, that's not the way it went down. Things still got very hairy for those first Christians. But they knew God has a reason for everything, and that, in the end, everything was going to work out according to God's great plan. Do you know the same? Do you believe that no matter what happens, the good, the bad and the ugly, God will somehow work good from it? If so, then I would say that is something to be positive about!

When confronted with difficulties, do these two things:

1. Ask God what lesson He wants you to learn from this.

2. Try to envision the good God will bring from this situation. (Note: It may be something as simple as you growing in faith and trust. Don't always be looking for something super-sized. That's another thing the world tries to sell us on – in order to have value, everything needs to be big and grandiose. Though perfectly capable, God doesn't often do super-sized. He typically does small but mighty.)

There may come times when we feel as if we just can't go on. It happens. Sometimes we allow the weight of the world to pull us down. We feel as though we have found ourselves in the middle of an episode of Mission: Impossible. If you feel that way, think about this: every time they had a mission to accomplish on Mission: Impossible, in the end they accomplished the mission. It turns out the missions weren't really impossible after all. (Gee, suddenly I feel cheated.) So, they got the job done, and they were just a bunch of human beings. Imagine if Almighty God had been involved in the mission! Now imagine this: Almighty God IS involved in the mission of your life. If you truly believe that God is with you (and I hope you do, because He is), then you must believe that anything is possible for you.

Jesus looked at them and said, "For human beings this is impossible, but for God all things are possible."
Matthew 19:26

Strength From Above

When I was growing up, my mom had a bunch of favorite sayings. Things like, "Go fly a kite!", "Go jump in a lake", "Take a long walk off a short pier" and "Go play in traffic" were standard fare around our house. I was always waiting for "Go stick a penny in a light socket," but that one never caught on. Now, before you go judging my mom as an unfit mother, you need to understand something. You see, Mom and Dad had six kids in a span of eight years. At any given time Mom had three in diapers. Then in the later years, they had six, count 'em SIX teenagers. Sanity in those days was surely elusive. Walk a mile in those shoes, my friend. I'm guessing you would come up with some choice sayings, too.

One of Mom's favorite sayings was really a prayer. And it was a prayer that was always answered. How do I know? Because Mom is still around to this day, and Mom is one of the most positive people I know. Mom would lift her eyes heavenward and cry, "Give me strength!" And while she may not have felt it at the moment, that strength always came. And it came from the source of all strength, Jesus Christ. The same source you and I can tap into every moment of every day and receive all the strength we need to accomplish whatever God wants us to accomplish.

I have the strength for everything through him
who empowers me.
Philippians 4:13

Lastly, we must remember that the things we think about are going to be the things we bring into our reality. We must always keep our minds focused on positive things. What we put into our minds is what is going to come out. If we keep feeding our mind with negative thoughts, then those negative thoughts will come out of us and we will attract negative things and negative people into our lives. This may sound like so much new age mumbo jumbo to some, but tell that to St. Paul. In his letter to the Philippians, he exhorted them to put only good stuff into their minds. We would do well to follow his advice.

Finally, brothers, whatever is true, whatever is honorable, whatever is just, whatever is pure, whatever is lovely, whatever is gracious, if there is any excellence and if there is anything worthy of praise, think about these things.
Philippians 4:8

I would like to offer a tip that has been very helpful to me in my struggle to keep my mind on positive things. It is an ancient practice. Whenever you find yourself drifting into negative thoughts, find a word or a phrase that will help snap your mind back to where it should be. Some people call this a mantra, others refer to it as a centering prayer. Call it what you will, but I have found it very helpful. There have been two that I have used throughout my life. The first is, "God, come to my assistance. Lord make haste to help me." (From the Liturgy of the Hours) The other is, "Son of David, have pity on me." (Mark 10:48) These brief little prayers are reminders to me that I need to rethink my thinking. Find a word or phrase that you are comfortable with and use it throughout the day to bring your mind back to excellent thoughts.

A positive attitude is one of the hallmarks of a Magnetic Christian. As you reflect on just the few Scripture passages I have presented here, I think you'll see that we can't not be positive about life! (How about that – using a double negative to encourage a positive.)

Questions for Reflection

1. How do I answer the question, "How are you?" How can I change my answer to reflect a more positive outlook on life?

2. What are my predominant thoughts and thought patterns? Do I keep my mind focused on good things?

3. Is there a word or phrase that I can use to keep me focused on positive things? Perhaps a favorite Scripture passage or prayer?

4. What are the five things for which I am most thankful? Write them down and recall one each time you find your thoughts turning negative.

5. Is there a time in my life when God turned something that seemed very negative at the time into something positive? How can I better envision the positive outcomes that God wants to bring from every situation in life?

Prayer

Father, you know that we can be so negative. Forgive us for the times when we only see the darkness. Help us to keep our minds focused on your goodness, and to share a positive attitude with a world that so desperately needs it. Amen.

CHAPTER TWO

ENTHUSIASM

Come and hear, all you who fear God,
while I recount what has been done for me.
I called to the Lord with my mouth;
praise was upon my tongue.
Psalm 66:16-17

Have you ever bought something from a salesperson? Of course you have; we all have. We all shop in slightly different ways. Some people do copious amounts of research before making even the smallest purchase. They come to the table armed to the teeth with information. They know what they want and how much they are willing to pay for it. Others play things a bit more by ear. They have general ideas about their purchase, but they can be swayed one way or another. Regardless of their style, both customers still have to engage in the sales game. Most people find that to be a daunting task. Why? Because many people look at sales people as untrustworthy. They view them as just out to make a buck. Someone who just wants to separate them from their money to get a commission.

The good sales person knows all of this. So the good

sales person employs techniques that will help put the customer at ease. In fact, all of the attributes you read about in this book are things that any good sales person will portray. That makes perfect sense because, like it or not, we are all sales people. While we may not do it as a profession, we are all selling something. And that something is ourselves. Every good sales person knows that no matter how wonderful their product is, the first thing they have to do is to sell themselves.

This is all the more important for the Magnetic Christian. There are an awful lot of people out there nowadays who look at Christians with a wary eye. For many, Christians are viewed as judgmental separatists. If you don't think the way we think and look the way we look and act the way that we tell you to act, then you can't be part of the club! While that may not be entirely accurate, perception is reality. If someone perceives Christians that way, then that is their reality. The question then becomes what are we doing to eliminate this perception?

Back to the sales analogy. I spent some years in the sales game. I have been a sales manager and a sales trainer. I've been on both sides of the fence. And I have found that the one attribute that will sell more than anything is enthusiasm. A sales person can have all the product knowledge in the world, but if they aren't enthusiastic about their product, they will invariably be looking for work elsewhere at some point. The same is true for the Magnetic Christian. (Well, not the part about being out of work. Trust me, God will never fire you. There is PLENTY of work to do in God's vineyard. We are the ones who quit.)

It's a universal principle. You've probably experienced it many times in your life. In fact, you've probably done a wonderful sales job on someone else because of your enthusiasm!

Word of Mouth

Remember the last time you discovered a really great restaurant? What did you do afterwards? Chances are you told some of your family and friends about how great the food was and what a nice experience you had. Smart companies know that kind of advertising is worth more than all of the great television and radio and Internet ads in the world. Nothing beats word of mouth advertising. On my radio show, I encourage my listeners every day to tell a friend about Seize the Day. Because I, too, know that a personal recommendation from a friend carries more weight than any other kind of advertising or sales pitch.

Does the Church need to be more involved in the many different means of getting the word out? Absolutely. And many churches are doing a fine job of it. More and more, you see billboards for different churches as you drive the highways and byways of America. TV ads and YouTube sermons will surely draw people's attention. But no matter how good those things are, none of them will ever come close to a personal invitation.

One of my all-time favorite TV characters was someone

you never saw on a sitcom or soap opera or drama. He was a pitch man named Billy Mays. I'm sure you saw him, probably thousands of times, before he died. With his trademark blue shirt (notice the "blue collar" kind of guy he was), black beard and booming voice, it was Billy Mays' enthusiasm that sold billions of dollars worth of products. I'm not saying we need to imitate Billy Mays' style, but can you imagine how we could change the world if we only exuded a fraction of his enthusiasm?

I remember recently going with my bride to see a movie that really surprised me. It wasn't advertised heavily, so not a lot of people knew about it. As soon as Michelle and I got out of the theater I was on my phone calling at least three friends I knew would love the movie. I was so enthusiastic that I couldn't wait to share it with my friends. Later that day I even went and put the trailer on my web site and Facebook page. A few days later some of those friends called me to thank me for the recommendation. My enthusiasm sold the movie.

It seems we're always eager to share our experiences about a great restaurant, movie, YouTube video, web site, etc. How much do you think we could change the world if we were so enthusiastic about God?

Do not grow slack in zeal, be fervent in spirit,
serve the LORD.
Romans 12:11

Yet it seems that not so many people have the same kind

of enthusiasm for God. But why? What is it that tempers our enthusiasm for sharing our faith? I suppose there are any number of answers to that question, but I believe it can all be summed up in one word: FEAR. And I believe the greatest fear we have in this area is the fear of rejection.

One of the greatest desires of human beings is acceptance. We all want to be liked. We all want to be loved. We all want to fit in. No one likes rejection. That's why so many people would never dream of working in sales. But any good sales manager will tell the sales people that people are not rejecting them, they are rejecting the offer. You can't take it personally. I believe the same is true with sharing our faith. Some people will be very open to hearing your story. For others, it may not be their time. But they won't be rejecting you, they'll be rejecting your offer. That's okay. It is absolutely not a reflection on you. Who knows, the seeds you plant in someone's heart today may take root some other time. The farmer doesn't hold back from planting the seeds just because the soil may be dry that day. God will provide the right conditions in His good time. But the seeds must be planted and ready.

> **MAGNETIC INSIGHT:**
> *Who knows, the seeds you plant in someone's heart today may take root some other time. God will provide the right conditions in His good time. But the seeds must be planted and ready.*

*Now who is going to harm you if you are
enthusiastic for what is good?*
1 Peter 3:13

Believing in Your Product

The biggest factor in engendering enthusiasm is belief in one's product or service. Let me ask you a question: would you be more or less inclined to buy a Ford car from a salesman who drove onto the lot in his Toyota? For me the answer would be less inclined. I mean, if the guy is trying to sell me a Ford, why wouldn't he be driving a Ford? Does he know something I don't? Does he not believe in his product enough to drive one himself?

As Magnetic Christians, what about our "product?" Is there anything better than eternal life with God through Jesus Christ? If you answered yes, then I suggest a check-up from the neck up. There are a lot of things in life to be enthusiastic about. We have great enthusiasm about our favorite sports team, a new house, car, boat or other toy, a raise or promotion at work, a new job...the list goes on and on. (Don't even get me started on how Americans worship sports. Sports fans are some of the most rabid and enthusiastic people I know. Imagine if we could harness just a fraction of the sports enthusiasm in America today and channel it for God!) But none of these even come close to comparing with having a relationship with Almighty God! Think about it – the Creator of the Universe offers us peace, love, joy, forgiveness, eternal life! How can we not be enthusiastic about that??

Be eager to present yourself as acceptable to God,
a workman who causes no disgrace,
imparting the word of truth without deviation.
2 Timothy 2:15

In the late 1980s, I met an evangelist who liked to refer to himself as a cheerleader for God. Charlie Osbourne was about as far away from looking like a cheerleader as anyone you would ever meet. After all, cheerleaders are young, fit, curvaceous

MAGNETIC INSIGHT:
The more enthusiastic we are about our faith, the more people will be drawn to Christ. Enthusiasm is contagious!

and toned. No offense, but Charlie was none of these. In fact, thinking of Charlie in a cheerleading outfit gives me the willies. Yet Charlie was perhaps the finest cheerleader I have ever met. He would get up on the stage and dance around and sing and, some would say, make an absolute fool of himself. But Charlie didn't care. He was a fool for Christ. And his enthusiasm was absolutely contagious! That man turned so many people on to God! And Charlie would always tell you that it wasn't about Charlie, it was about Jesus.

This is such an important point for the Magnetic Christian. We always have to walk a fine line between drawing people to ourselves and drawing them to Christ. Many people will use this as an excuse to not share their faith. "Oh," they'll say, "I'm not comfortable talking about myself," or "I don't want this to be all about me. That's so vain." But you must remember, many people will not see Christ unless they see Him in you. And that means you have to share part of you. I believe Jesus spoke clearly about this.

"You are the light of the world. A city set on a mountain cannot be hidden. Nor do they light a lamp and then put it under a bushel basket; it is set on a lampstand, where it gives light to all in the house. Just so, your light must shine before others, that they may see your good deeds and glorify your heavenly Father."
Matthew 5:14-16

Warning! Warning!

I'm always a bit skeptical when someone starts a sentence with, "God wants you to…" I mean, how do they know what God wants me to do? Does God really want me to send them money, buy their product, email my friends about them, etc.? That's a pretty bold way to start a sentence. That being said, I'm going to do it right now. God wants you to be enthusiastic about your faith. How do I know this? Because He says so! He also gives us a warning about what will happen if we are not enthusiastic.

"The Amen, the faithful and true witness, the source of God's creation, says this: 'I know your works; I know that you are neither cold nor hot. I wish you were either cold or hot. So, because you are lukewarm, neither hot nor cold, I will spit you out of my mouth. For you say, "I am rich and affluent and have no need of anything," and yet do not realize that you are wretched, pitiable, poor, blind and naked. I advise you to buy from me gold refined by fire so that you

may be rich, and white garments to put on so that your
shameful nakedness may not be exposed, and buy ointment
to smear on your eyes so that you may see. Those whom I
love, I reprove and chastise. Be earnest, therefore, and re-
pent. Behold, I stand at the door and knock. If anyone hears
my voice and opens the door, [then] I will enter his house
and dine with him, and he with me. I will give the victor the
right to sit with me on my throne, as I myself first won the
victory and sit with my Father on his throne.'"
Revelation 3:14-21

Notice in that passage the dire consequences of being lukewarm. Jesus will spit you out of His mouth! That doesn't sound like a very pleasant thing to me. So we know we need to be either cold or hot. The lukewarm, fence-sitting, just-dipping-your-toes-in-the-water thing just isn't going to cut it. We're either all in, or we're not in at all. I submit to you that Jesus wants us to be all in, HOT (read: enthusiastic) about our faith. I believe the words of Jesus bolster my position.

"I have come to set the earth on fire,
and how I wish it were already blazing!"
Luke 12:49

Is your heart blazing with love for Jesus? Or are you lukewarm? Let's pray that our hearts will be a veritable bonfire of love for God! The more enthusiastic we are about our faith, the more people will be drawn to Christ. Enthusiasm is contagious!

31

I've used a lot of sales imagery in this chapter. As I said early on, most people don't look too kindly on the sales profession. But think of it this way: in a good sales transaction, both sides win. Everyone gets what they want. It reminds me of the words of one of my heroes in the field of motivational speaking, Zig Ziglar. Zig always told people that they could have everything in life they wanted if they would just help enough other people get what they wanted. And what we all want is eternal happiness with God. Imagine…you can help someone find that. Now that's something to be enthusiastic about!

Questions for Reflection

1. Am I enthusiastic about my relationship with God?

2. Do I share my enthusiasm with others? How do I show it?

3. What are some ways that I can build my enthusiasm for my faith?

4. What are some things that are holding me back from sharing my enthusiasm for God?

5. Who are two or three friends or family members that I can share my enthusiasm with this week, and how can I do that?

Prayer

Father, help me to be enthusiastic about my faith. Reveal to me ways that I can share my enthusiasm with others, that they might see You through me. Amen.

CHAPTER THREE

FRIENDLINESS

A faithful friend is a sturdy shelter;
he who finds one finds a treasure.
A faithful friend is beyond price,
no sum can balance his worth.
A faithful friend is a life-saving remedy,
such as he who fears God finds;
For he who fears God behaves accordingly,
and his friend will be like himself.
Sirach 6:14-17

A young boy came home from his first day at a new school. His eyes were red and swollen; he had been crying. His mother met him at the door and gave him a big hug. She knew this would be a tough day for her son. While she really already knew the answer, she asked, "Well, how was your first day at school?"

"Not so good," came the reply.

"Tell me why, sweetheart."

"Nobody wants to be my friend. None of the other kids

would talk to me and nobody asked me to play with them at recess."

His mom asked, "Son, did you try talking to any of the other kids?"

"No," said the son, "I was waiting for them to talk to me."

His mom pulled her boy close and spoke softly to him. "Sweetie," she said, "Let me tell you something that my mommy told me a long time ago when we moved and I had to start at a new school. Mom always said, 'If you want to make a friend, be a friend.' Do you know what that means?"

Her son gave her a puzzled look and responded, "Not really, Mommy."

"It means if you want someone to be your friend, then you have to be friendly to them. People want to be friends with friendly people."

The next day the mom packed the boy some extra snacks in his lunch and told him to offer the extra snacks to some of the other kids in his class. He came home that afternoon and told his mom all about his new friends.

[This parable was brought to you by your friendly neighborhood bakery.]

What's the moral of this story for the Magnetic Christian? CARRY SNACKS! There's no easier way to draw people in than feeding them! (All of my Lutheran friends are nodding their heads in agreement right now.)

The mom's advice to her son was spot on. Friendliness is another hallmark of the Magnetic Christian. But friendliness can be hard to define. One person's definition of friendliness may differ from someone else's. What one person perceives to be friendly may be viewed as pushy to another. But there are some things I think most people would agree are part of friendliness. Perhaps the most common one can be found in the words of Jesus. We know it as the Golden Rule.

Do to others whatever you would have them do to you.
This is the law and the prophets.
Matthew 7:12

Interestingly, I have found that there are a lot of people who have no idea these words were spoken by Jesus. While it's great that Jesus elucidated this, He is not the first to have proposed the principle. Really, it is written on our hearts. It is a universal truth. If we just treat others the way we want to be treated, we'll have more friends than we know what to do with. In fact, think about your true friends. Do they not follow the Golden Rule with you? Sure they do! That's one of the reasons you're friends.

Endear yourself to the assembly;
before a ruler bow your head.
Give a hearing to the poor man,
and return his greeting with courtesy.
Sirach 4:7-8

Listen Up!

Another extremely important aspect of friendliness for the Magnetic Christian is listening. A true friend is a good listener. Have you ever been with someone who talks non-stop? Usually that non-stop talk centers around them. Or worse yet, it is nothing more than gossip. Gossip can be a sure-fire killer of real friendships. Why? Because the one who gossips TO you will undoubtedly gossip ABOUT you. Gossip must never be on the lips of the Magnetic Christian. I have found that relationships with non-stop talkers generally tend to be very short lived. As the person went on and on, I felt more and more as if they didn't really care about me. I felt like nothing more than a sounding board. That doesn't feel very good, does it?

Time for another guilty pleasure confession. I am a fan of Judge Judy. I used to feel a bit uneasy about that. Then I realized that ten million other people are in the same boat as me. So now I freely admit it. I watch Judge Judy. I even DVR it. While many of the folks in her court are goofballs, I really appreciate Judge Judy's no-nonsense wisdom. She often reminds the people in her court that God gave them two ears and one mouth and they need to use them in that proportion. Her point is that most people talk twice as much as they listen. Seems to me the world would probably be a better place if we turned that around. Good listeners make good friends.

I'd like to share a little advice from my professional life. I started in the radio business in 1979. Back in those days we used to spin 45s. (If you're not familiar with a 45, it was a black plastic disc a bit bigger than a CD with grooves on it that you played on a turntable. It got its name because the turntable rotated at 45 RPM. If I have to explain what a turntable is, I'm just going to go back to the old folks' home, thank you very much.) Anyway, in my many years on the radio I have interviewed hundreds, if not thousands, of people. When

> **MAGNETIC INSIGHT:** *Be a good listener. Let people talk. Hear them out. ASK QUESTIONS. And really listen to the answers. Make them feel valued.*

I first started, I used to make the biggest mistake that an interviewer can make. I bring this up because this is the same mistake that most people make even in casual conversation. When the person I was speaking to was talking, I wasn't listening. Instead I was thinking of the next question I was going to ask or a witty remark I thought I should make. I was a terrible listener. Because of that, many of my early interviews were less than stellar.

Don't make that mistake, Magnetic Christian. Be a good listener. Let people talk. Hear them out. ASK QUESTIONS. And really listen to the answers. Don't interrupt. Look people in the eye, lean forward a bit (but not into their space) and show them that you're truly interested and concerned about them and what they have to say. Make them feel valued.

I've encountered people who think that evangelization means spouting Bible verses at people and telling them what terrible sinners they are and that they're headed straight for hell if they don't shape up. What a turnoff! A friend would never do that. Now, I'm not saying we shouldn't tell people they are sinners. That is a fact we all have to face up to. I'm also not saying we should water down or dumb down the truth. That would be wrong, and would truly be doing a disservice. What I am saying is the way you tell someone is of the utmost importance. Always think of how you would treat a friend. And then try to treat everyone the same way.

Welcome anyone who is weak in faith.
Romans 14:1

You're Welcome!

A friendly person is a welcoming person. I was reading a recent study that said many young people leave a church because they don't find the people welcoming. They felt as though they were being judged. To be honest, I have found this notion is often, though not always, in peoples' heads. They have a preconceived notion that they are going to be judged. Perhaps they are feeling guilty about aspects of their own lives. Regardless of the objective reality of the situation, once again, perception is reality. If people perceive us as being unwelcoming or judgmental, we must ask ourselves why. We must first search our hearts and see if we truly are that way. And if we are, then we must pray for the grace to repent. Remember, the Church is not a museum for saints, it is a hospital for sinners.

Have you ever been to a place where you haven't felt welcome? Why was that? What was it that made you feel unwelcome? I suspect the main reason was probably much like our story about the young boy's first day at a new school. Nobody would talk to him. I can't tell you how many times I have been to a church where nobody spoke to me or even so much as looked at me. Many churches certainly need to do a better job of making newcomers feel welcome. But as Magnetic Christians, we can't leave that up to the church or the ushers or the welcoming committee. It has to start with us. Start looking for opportunities to welcome people. Make it a point to smile and shake hands with someone you haven't met before. Tell them your name, and ask theirs. This is one of the most effective ways to start building a relationship. People are flattered when you call them by name. Don't leave this practice of welcoming at church. Take it with you wherever you go. It will serve you well in every area of your life.

Speaking of...

The final stop on our friendliness tour is – the mouth.

A kind mouth multiplies friends,
and gracious lips prompt friendly greetings.
Sirach 6:5

Words are powerful. While the old axiom "The pen is mightier than the sword" is certainly true, I believe the spoken word contains even greater power. It is a power that we far too often take lightly or even abuse.

Have you ever hurt someone with your words? Of course you have. We all have. Interestingly, even Jesus hurt some people with His words. The scribes and Pharisees were none too happy about being called hypocrites, blind guides and a brood of vipers.

Go back in your mind for a moment. Can you remember a time when a parent or family member hurt you with their words? As a father, I am all too familiar with this phenomenon. While I have always tried my best to be a positive person, my kids seem to remember every negative thing I ever uttered to them. Most of the things I

MAGNETIC INSIGHT:
The Magnetic Christian must speak words of peace, love, welcoming, understanding, patience and encouragement.

have absolutely no recollection of. But they sure do. I don't say this as a knock on my kids. I tell this story to illustrate the power of words, especially negative words. A wound inflicted with words can often be a lifelong wound.

One of the problems with words is that once they are out, you can never take them back. Oh, you can say, "I take that back." You can say it a million times. But it can never happen. This is why the Magnetic Christian is very careful with words. Jesus spoke clearly about the revealing power of words.

He summoned the crowd and said to them, "Hear and understand. It is not what enters one's mouth that defiles that person; but what comes out of the mouth is what defiles

one. But the things that come out of the mouth
come from the heart, and they defile."
Matthew 15:10-11, 18

The Magnetic Christian must speak words of peace, love, welcoming, understanding, patience and encouragement. I realize this is not always easy. Especially in stressful situations, we may have a tendency to pop off without thinking. Those are the times when we will most likely say words that wound. The Scriptures give us a wonderful example of how we can avoid that.

In Nehemiah 2, there is a story of how Nehemiah wants to ask his king if he can go back to Judah to rebuild his ancestral city. The king asks, "What is it, then, that you wish?" Nehemiah recounts, "I prayed to the God of heaven and then answered the king." Before he opened his mouth, he prayed. What a novel concept! How different would our approach to things be if we just said a quick prayer before we opened our mouths? If we just allow the Holy Spirit to do more of the talking, I think we'll see a world of difference.

St. James spoke clearly about the power of the tongue.

Consider how small a fire can set a huge forest ablaze.
The tongue is also a fire. It exists among our members as
a world of malice, defiling the whole body and setting the
entire course of our lives on fire, itself set on fire by Ge-
henna. For every kind of beast and bird, of reptile and sea

creature, can be tamed and has been tamed by the human species, but no human being can tame the tongue. It is a restless evil, full of deadly poison. With it we bless the Lord and Father, and with it we curse human beings who are made in the likeness of God. From the same mouth come blessing and cursing. This need not be so, my brothers.
James 3:5-10

Notice in that passage that St. James says no human being can tame the tongue. True enough. But we know that with God, all things are possible, including the taming of the human tongue. Ask God to tame your tongue. Ask for the grace to use your tongue for blessing, and not for cursing. That's what a friend would do.

You've heard the old saying, cleanliness is next to godliness. (I really think that someone's mom made that up to get her kids to clean up their rooms. I don't have any proof of that, but that's my suspicion.) For the Magnetic Christian, I would make a slight change to that saying.

Friendliness is next to godliness.

Questions for Reflection
1. What are some things that I find attractive about my friends?

2. When others are talking, what can I do to let them know that I am truly listening?

3. When at church, am I welcoming? Are there people

that I have been sitting near for years that I don't even know their names? Am I willing to step out of my comfort zone and introduce myself to others, especially strangers?

4. Who have I wounded with my words? Parents? Children? Siblings? Co-workers? What can I do to rectify those situations?

5. Is there someone in my life with whom I have not been particularly friendly? If so, why? What steps can I take this week to be a better friend to all?

Prayer

Father, help me to be friendly and welcoming, especially to those who feel alienated. Give me the grace to be a friend to all. Amen.

CHAPTER FOUR

CONFIDENCE

Thus we may say with confidence:
"The Lord is my helper,
[and] I will not be afraid.
What can anyone do to me?"
Hebrews 13:6

Two outs, bottom of the ninth, bases loaded, down by three. Up to the plate strides the batter. Eyes intense, chest out, bat at the ready. You know it, he knows it, everyone in the park feels it. There's a grand slam sitting on the barrel of that bat.

She enters the room and a hush falls over the standing room only audience. She strides up to the podium, surveys the room and pauses. As she smiles and begins to speak, it's so quiet you can hear the blood swishing in your own ears.

A doctor walks into a side room. A family awaits word. The doctor relates that it is worse than he thought. The cancer has spread. The wife looks at him resolutely and says, "Not to worry, doctor. We're going to win this battle. God will see us through it."

A young boy picks up a stone from his belt. He loads it into his sling as the giant man a few yards away chides him. All of the boy's people are cowering in fear. Yet the wiry boy tells the behemoth that he is about to go down. David fires the stone from his sling and Goliath hits the dirt.

> **MAGNETIC INSIGHT:**
> *When we put our trust, our hope, our belief in God, only then can we truly have confidence. This is because we are relying on God, and not on ourselves.*

What is it that the characters in these stories have? Are they smarter than everyone else? Are they the biggest, fastest, strongest? Maybe they have ESP. Or in the case of the baseball player, ESPN. No, these people all have what every Magnetic Christian should have: Confidence.

Beloved, if [our] hearts do not condemn us, we have confidence in God and receive from him whatever we ask, because we keep his commandments and do what pleases him.
1 John 3:21-22

Confidence is, at its core, simply belief. Belief that a desired result is going to come about. But for the Magnetic Christian, it goes far beyond that. It is a belief that God is in control, and that He is the one who will bring about the desired result. True confidence is knowing that God's will will be done. We must always be careful how we view this, though.

Most self-help books will talk of self-confidence and self-esteem. While these are certainly good and necessary things to have, they are not self standing. Self-confidence and self-esteem are simply byproducts of confidence and trust in God. When we put our trust, our hope, our belief in God, only then can we truly have confidence. This is because we are relying on God, and not on ourselves. You can always tell when someone is relying on oneself because their "confidence" is usually just cockiness - and cockiness is not really confidence at all. Usually cockiness is simply a defense mechanism of someone who is really unsure and insecure. The Magnetic Christian has no use for those things.

The Scriptures speak again and again about how our confidence is derived from God.

For the LORD will be your confidence,
and will keep your foot from the snare.
Proverbs 3:26

Confidence = Fearlessness

A first cousin of confidence is fearlessness. One could write volumes of books about that subject alone. I am including fearlessness under the heading of confidence, because the one who exudes confidence will also be fearless. When it comes to fear (as in not having it), we find a Scriptural bonanza! In fact, the admonition "Be not afraid" (or some variation thereof) is the most common admonition in the Bible. It is spoken by God the Father, Jesus Christ, angels and humans.

47

The LORD is my light and my salvation;
whom do I fear?
The LORD is my life's refuge;
of whom am I afraid?
When evildoers come at me
to devour my flesh,
These my enemies and foes
themselves stumble and fall.
Though an army encamp against me,
my heart does not fear;
Though war be waged against me,
even then do I trust.
Psalm 27:1-3

When the disciples saw him walking on the sea
they were terrified. "It is a ghost," they said, and they cried
out in fear. At once [Jesus] spoke to them, "Take courage,
it is I; do not be afraid."
Matthew 14:26-27

There is no fear in love, but perfect love drives out fear be-
cause fear has to do with punishment, and so the one who
fears is not yet perfect in love.
1 John 4:18

A number of years ago I was working at Spirit FM in
Tampa, FL. On occasion we would have up and coming mu-
sicians stop by the studio to promote a new record. It was
nice, because we had the opportunity to just hang out with
them for a while and get to know them. I remember one particular day when a young artist named Nate dropped by un-

announced. He happened to be in the area and just wanted to meet the staff and chat. He was still trying to make his mark in the industry, or so I thought. Nate was in his early to mid twenties, young enough to be my son. But his youth belied his wisdom.

Nate said, "I'm really just living my life without fear. I figure that, until God is ready to call me home, I'm bulletproof."

Now, some people could certainly take that the wrong way. That statement may seem like cockiness bordering on foolishness. But I got it right away, and it helped to change the way that I think. Nate didn't mean that he could jump in front of a freight train and he wouldn't get smooshed. No, that would be foolish. What he meant was that God had a perfect plan for his life, and until that plan was carried out in its fullness, there was nothing anyone could do to Nate that was outside of God's plan. He had no need to succumb to fear. I hope this makes sense. Let me reiterate, this kind of confidence does not give us license to be foolish. But Nate was living his life with the confident assurance that God was watching over him. And the same is true for you!

God indeed is my savior;
I am confident and unafraid.
My strength and my courage is the LORD,
and he has been my savior.
Isaiah 12:2

FEAR
I want to go a bit deeper into this notion of fear, because

fear is the enemy of confidence. Actually, fear is the enemy of all the attributes of the Magnetic Christian. In fact, I believe that fear is of the devil. But before we go further, let me clarify. There is fear that is healthy. For instance, if you find yourself in a situation where your life, health or safety are threatened, fear will kick in. This is a healthy fear. This ignites your "fight or flight" mechanism. This is the kind of fear that is not only good, but necessary. But this is not the fear of which we speak. The unhealthy kind of fear can be thought of through this acronym:

False
Evidence
Appearing
Real

Let me give an example. We'll go back to an earlier thought where we talked about fear of rejection. Let's say you've been asked to speak in front of a group of people. If you're like most people, you break out in a cold sweat at the very thought. (Side note: In a survey done many years ago, the fear of public speaking was, for most people, greater than the fear of death. It's not a very popular activity.) Reluctantly, you agree. You do your research and prepare assiduously. Finally the big day arrives. As you wait in the wings, suddenly a wave of fear washes over you. You begin to sweat; your heart races and your legs go numb. Why, you're not even sure you can make it to the dais, much less talk! Sound familiar? So why does this happen?

You have already made up your mind that you are going to bomb. You're worried about forgetting your material, stumbling over words; you begin playing out every worst case scenario that could occur. You have already decided the audience will reject you. Remember the acronym? False Evidence Appearing Real. There is absolutely no evidence that you are going to bomb. It is false. You manufactured that evidence in your own mind. Because of that, it appears real - to you. I can assure you, as someone who has been a public speaker all of my life, the audience is rooting for you. They want you to succeed! The same is true for God. God wants you to succeed! (Recall Jeremiah 29:11)

MAGNETIC INSIGHT: *Instead of centering on "I," center your affirmation on God, and God's power working through you.*

Let's take this to a more personal level of sharing your faith, of telling someone about your relationship with God. Our initial fear is that we will be judged. We're afraid that the person to whom we're speaking, whether friend, foe or somewhere in between, will think we're some kind of nutbag, a Jesus freak. In essence, we're afraid of what they will think of us. In reality, that fear exists only in our mind. It is not real or rational. But because we have placed it there, it is our reality. It is only when we begin to recognize this needless fear creeping into our heads that we can begin to let God take control over it. We begin to change our perception, which in turn will change our reality.

Affirmations

I want to offer a bit of help if you have trouble with confidence. In the chapter on Positivity, we talked about mantras, or short words, phrases or sentences that will help bring your mind back to positive things when you find you are falling into negative thought patterns. Affirmations are very similar. Affirmations are words, phrases or even Scripture verses that we say to ourselves to bolster our confidence, to bring us back to reality when we find ourselves succumbing to our fears. They need to be positive and affirming. Of course, you can make up your own. Many positive mental attitude gurus will tell you to make them personal, using "I" phrases. For instance, "I am strong!" or "I am confident!" or "I am a great public speaker!" These are all fine and good. They do, indeed, help bolster our confidence. But I would like to suggest a slightly different affirmation process.

Instead of centering on "I," center your affirmation on God, and God's power working through you. Because no matter how good or strong or confident you think you are, you've got nothing on God. Here are a few of my suggestions for great affirmations:

"God is with me!"

"Be not afraid!"

"God is my refuge and my strength!" (From Psalm 46:1)

"Jesus, I trust in you."

"I can do all things through Christ who strengthens me!"
(Philippians 4:13)

Of course, your options are limitless. Search the Scriptures and see if certain phrases pop out at you. (Hint: the Psalms are a great place to look.) The key is to keep it short and sweet and always have it at the ready. Let your affirmation bring you back to the knowledge that God is on your side, ready to give you all the confidence you need in every situation.

Visualize This

Another great way to help us overcome unnecessary fear is visualization. Visualization is a technique that is used by most all high performing people. Most every world-class athlete uses visualization. It is simply using the power of your imagination to see the desired result. For example, a professional golfer will, before striking the ball, see the ball in his or her mind flying off the club head and going exactly where they want it to go. They see the shape of the shot, the spin on the ball and the way they want it to land. In our public speaking example, you would visualize the audience attentively hanging on your every word. At the end of your talk, they rise in unison and give you a standing ovation. When visualizing, be very detailed. See the smiles on the faces of your audience. Notice them leaning forward in their seats. Visualize them asking questions after your presentation. Then live it.

Please don't think this is only about public speaking or golf or athletics. We're just using those as an example. This will work in every area of your life, including sharing your faith. Before you talk with a person or a group, see them nodding in approval, anxious to hear more about God's goodness. If you truly believe that God wants you to succeed in whatever it is you do, and that God has your back, then you can go into any situation in life brimming with confidence! See yourself as God sees you – a champion, a hero, a child of His!

For God did not give us a spirit of cowardice
but rather of power and love and self-control.
So do not be ashamed of your testimony to our Lord.
2 Timothy 1:7-8

Confidence is a very attractive quality, and one the Magnetic Christian should always have. Perhaps the most important thing to remember is that confidence is something that we not only must have with people, but especially with God. There is no need for us to be timid, because we have confidence in and through Christ Jesus. St. John was big on this idea.

And we have this confidence in him, that if we ask anything
according to his will, he hears us.
1 John 5:14

Go back to the story of David and Goliath, which you can read in 1 Samuel 17. From all indications, David had absolutely no right to be confident. He was going up against a giant, a man who mowed down everyone who got in his way. Goliath was bigger, badder, stronger and better armed than the young David. Yet David was supremely confident. He KNEW he was going to slay the giant. How? David KNEW that God was with him! I hope you KNOW the very same thing. God is with you, and wants to give you everything you need to be successful in every area of life, and to help build up the Kingdom of God. Carry that thought with you always and you can go into any situation with confidence!

Questions for Reflection

1. Who are some examples of confident people in my life? Think about common traits that these people have.

2. What are my biggest fears in life?

3. How are these fears holding me back from being all that God wants me to be?

4. What are some specific situations where I lack confidence?

5. What steps can I take in the coming days and weeks to help build my confidence? (Hint: prayer and Scripture reflection will help!)

Prayer

Father, I believe that you are with me. Help me to always keep this thought close to my heart, that I may have confidence to boldly do your work in the world. Amen.

CHAPTER FIVE

HUMILITY

And all of you, clothe yourselves with humility
in your dealings with one another, for:
"God opposes the proud
but bestows favor on the humble."
So humble yourselves under the mighty hand of God,
that he may exalt you in due time.
1 Peter 5:5-6

I once asked a guy what he thought his greatest asset was. "Oh," he replied, "Definitely my humility!" Buh-dum bum! Kind of shot himself in the foot with that answer, wouldn't you say?

Humility is one of those funny things that can be hard to qualify, tough to define. In the story above, the guy disqualified himself immediately. Why? Because someone who has humility is someone who would never admit to having humility! Interesting principle if you think about it. So what is humility? How would you define it?

Here is how the *Merriam-Webster Collegiate Dictionay* defines humble: Humble - adj. – not proud or haughty, not arrogant or assertive. Lacking all signs of pride, aggressiveness, or self-assertiveness.

That's an interesting definition, isn't it? It actually doesn't say what "humble" is. It only tells us what it isn't. I suppose if we use that definition as a guide, we could put it into a number of "uns," or negative terms. Humility is UN-proud, UN-haughty, UN-arrogant, UN-assertive. Eh…I don't know about you, but that doesn't work so well for me. It's like saying, "I don't know what humility is, but I know what it isn't."

I want to propose a quick exercise for you. Put this book down and see if you can put into words what humility is. Perhaps you can think of someone you know who is humble and describe attributes or behaviors that person exhibits. Try it now.

So…how did you do? Did you find it difficult to put into words? If you did, trust me that you're not alone. Luckily, I have some help for us! That help can be found on the pages of Scripture. There are so many passages in Scripture that speak of humility. Most of them use the words humble and humility without really describing what it is. I have found three specific passages I think will help us get a real handle on what humility is, and how we, as Magnetic Christians, can practice it in our lives.

The Humility of Christ

Do nothing out of selfishness or out of vainglory; rather,
humbly regard others as more important than yourselves,
each looking out not for his own interests, but [also]
everyone for those of others. Have among yourselves
the same attitude that is also yours in Christ Jesus,
Who, though he was in the form of God, did not regard
equality with God something to be grasped.
Philippians 2:3-6

Here are some key attributes of humility from this passage:

Selfless
Not vain
Looking out for the interests of others, and not self
Christ-like

Let's break these down and briefly discuss each of them.
The humble are selfless. They have come to the understanding that the world does not revolve around them and their needs and desires. Humility naturally de-

> **MAGNETIC INSIGHT:**
> *The humble person is not self-centered, but other-centered.*

flects attention away from the self. Humility causes us to be other-centered, not self-centered. How many humble people do you know that constantly want to draw attention to themselves? As is the case with all the Magnetic Christian's attributes, Jesus is the perfect example. As we see in the passage above, Christ Jesus knew full well of His divine nature. Yet

He never flaunted it. In fact, He often told people not to tell anyone else about who He really was. Jesus knew that the Father knew His heart. That was enough for Him. So it is for the Magnetic Christian. There is no need to go blowing one's horn, seeking the attention of others. God knows what you're all about. Leave it at that.

Vanity and humility are mutually exclusive. Vanity is the mechanism we use to seek attention. Before we go on, I want to make a distinction. Wanting to look nice, dress nice and be presentable are good things. Vanity is not necessarily about the clothes we wear, our hairdo and makeup or how we want our bodies to look. Vanity is a matter of the heart. A humble person is not a vain person. Vanity is really a form of self-ishness. We all have flaws – in our appearance and our per-sonalities. Constantly chasing after "perfection" as the world defines it will do nothing more than leave us empty, because we will never achieve it. I believe that when the motiva-tion for our appearance is specifically to draw attention to ourselves or to outdo others, then we have crossed the line into vanity. The Magnetic Christian must always be wary of vanity or vainglory.

As mentioned above, the humble are not self-centered, but other-centered. They are concerned about the well be-ing of others. They are the ones who go out of their way to make others feel comfortable when in uncomfortable situa-tions. This is because the humble don't really give a flying fig about what other people think of them. Instead of try-ing to keep up with the Joneses, the humble person wants to make sure that the Joneses have all they need, including love and friendship. The humble person is actually happy for the Joneses' success!

While the humble may have a competitive spirit, that spirit of competition is always directed at doing the best they can, and is not directed at crushing their opponent. Perhaps you've seen professional athletes that struck you as humble. If so, it's probably because they didn't take inordinate pleasure in defeating their opponent, but because they were happy that their hard work and the hard work of their team paid off in a victory. The humble person is always gracious in victory and defeat.

Humility and Love

The next place we'll go in Scripture speaks of these same things. You may be familiar with it. If you have ever been to a wedding, chances are pretty good you've heard it. It is often referred to as "The Love Chapter." In 1 Corinthians 13, St. Paul talks about love. He describes what love is, and what it isn't. Read through this passage once. Then read through it a second time, but make one change. When you read through it the second time, substitute the word "humility" for "love.

Love is patient, love is kind. It is not jealous,
[love] is not pompous, it is not inflated, it is not rude,
it does not seek its own interests,
it is not quick-tempered, it does not brood over injury,
it does not rejoice over wrongdoing
but rejoices with the truth.
1 Corinthians 13:4-6

It really works, doesn't it? It seems that humility and love must be very closely related. Indeed, they are. Humility mirrors all of the attributes of love we read about in 1 Corinthians 13. There is another attribute of humility not mentioned in this passage that I think is closely related - meekness. In the Sermon on the Mount, Jesus said, "Blessed are the meek, for they will inherit the land." (Matthew 5:5) Unfortunately, in the minds of many, meekness equals weakness. This is not a quality that is popular in the world today.

I mention this because it seems to me that, especially of late, humility is frowned upon in our culture. The world tells us these days that one must always show "strength." Humility is for losers. But this "strength," which manifests itself in smack talk and bravado, is really false strength. Real strength flourishes in humility, because real strength shows itself through self-control, which shines through in humility. The Magnetic Christian understands that meekness is not weakness. On the contrary, we are called to imitate Christ, who said, "Take my yoke upon you and learn from me, for I am meek and humble of heart." (Matthew 11:29) Christ shows us that there is strength in meekness and humility.

Learning Humility from a Tax Collector

We see a very intimate portrait of humility (and lack thereof) in our next Scripture passage.

He then addressed this parable to those who were convinced of their own righteousness and despised everyone else. "Two people went into the temple area to pray; one was a Pharisee and the other was a tax collector. The

Pharisee took up his position and spoke this prayer to himself, 'O God, I thank you that I am not like the rest of humanity – greedy, dishonest, adulterous – or even like this tax collector. I fast twice a week, and I pay tithes on my whole income.' But the tax collector stood off at a distance and would not even raise his eyes to heaven but beat his breast and prayed, 'O God, be merciful to me a sinner.' I tell you, the latter went home justified, not the former; for everyone who exalts himself will be humbled, and the one who humbles himself will be exalted."

Luke 18:9-14

So how do we boil this down? The introductory sentence to Jesus' parable speaks volumes. Those who are humble are not "convinced of their own righteousness." In other words, the humble recognize their own littleness, their own sinfulness. They are able to stop pretending that they are perfect or without fault, stop blaming others for their own faults and accept responsibility for their actions. And rather than looking askance at fellow sinners, they can look at other sinners and live by the old credo, "There but for the grace of God go I."

This always reminds me of a story about Archbishop Fulton Sheen. Archbishop Sheen was celebrating Mass in a prison on Christmas Day. At the beginning of his homily, he looked over the inmates and said, "The only difference between you and me is that you got caught." While Archbishop Sheen may not have actually committed any criminal acts that would land him behind bars, his point was made. We are all sinners, saved by grace. Some people recognize that fact, others don't. The humble realize they are always just one step away from falling off a precipice. The opportunity and enticement to sin are always lurking around every corner. No one is immune to the allure of sin. Humility calls us to recognize that, to be vigilant, and to have compassion for those who do fall.

Like the tax collector, the humble know they have no business even calling out to, much less being in the presence of a holy God. Yet they also understand God's amazing love and grace. While we are certainly not worthy, God welcomes us anyway, because we are made worthy through the blood of Jesus. That's good news!

The Pharisee, on the other hand, lacked all humility. Why? First, because he wasn't afraid to blow his own horn, even to the point of thinking he could put one over on God Himself! The Pharisee had deluded himself, convincing himself that he was all that (and a bag of chips, if they had bags of chips back then). And the fact that he had no qualms about voicing his self-inflated opinion made for proof positive of his lack of humility. The Magnetic Christian has no need of this. God sees and knows all we do. There is no need to try to convince anyone of our greatness. We do the things we do out of love for God and others, not to garner accolades and acceptance of people. The humble person is soft-spoken and gentle. Second, and worst of all, the Pharisee looked upon the tax collector as lower than himself, perhaps even sub-human. He had fallen head over heels into the sin of pride.

Pride is the antithesis of humility. Pride causes us to look down on others, to think we are better than others. Pride is the deadliest of sins.

You Can't Fake It

There are those who think humility can be faked. False humility can actually be a dangerous thing, and the Magnetic Christian must never fall into this trap. Here's how it works: we berate ourselves and denigrate ourselves, often using an "Aw, shucks!" attitude. It often sounds like this: "Oh, it was nothing. I'm really not very good at that at all. It was just dumb luck. Anyone could have done it." Of course, what's really happening is we are fishing for compliments. We want people to disagree with us. We want them to tell us how wonderful we are. I get it. I would be lying if I said that I haven't used those kinds of tactics in the past. If you find yourself going down that road, put on the brakes pronto.

> **MAGNETIC INSIGHT:**
> *The truly humble know that they have strengths and weaknesses. They are not afraid to admit it, and are willing to let God use both.*

> *My son, conduct your affairs with humility,*
> *and you will be loved more than a giver of gifts.*
> *Humble yourself the more, the greater you are,*
> *and you will find favor with God. For great is the power of*
> *God; by the humble he is glorified.*
> **Sirach 3:17-19**

You see, while humility and love are very closely related, true humility also has a large dose of confidence in it. I believe true humility lies in recognizing the gifts that God has given us and not trying to downplay them. Rather, give the credit where the credit is due – to God! By showing false humility and being self-deprecating, we actually do a disservice to God. This, of course, can be a fine line to walk at times. But the truly humble know that they have strengths and weaknesses. They are not afraid to admit it, and are willing to let God use both.

Who among you is wise and understanding?
Let him show his works by a good life in the humility
that comes from wisdom.
James 3:13

Finally, I would like to mention something I think a lot of people struggle with when it comes to humility: taking a compliment. While we should never fish for compliments, they will invariably come our way when we are helping others and doing God's work. Too many people think that part of humility is deflecting compliments or telling others they are wrong to compliment them. While you may genuinely feel that way, I believe it is the wrong way to go about accepting a compliment. I think the best way to accept a compliment is to simply say, "Thank you." And, again, to give the credit to God. After all, if it weren't for God giving you the talent or the gift or the wherewithal to do whatever you did, you never could have done it in the first place!

Finally, all of you, be of one mind, sympathetic, loving

toward one another, compassionate, humble.
Do not return evil for evil, or insult for insult;
but, on the contrary, a blessing, because to this
you were called, that you might inherit a blessing.
1 Peter 3:8-9

Questions for Reflection

1. Would other people look at me as humble? (Be honest in your assessment.) If not, why not?

2. Do I take compliments well? If not, how or what can I do better?

3. Read over 1 Corinthians 13 again. Go through each of the attributes that St. Paul gives to love, and ask yourself how you could improve on each in your own life. (Example: Am I patient? Am I kind? Am I jealous?)

4. Am I strong enough to be meek? How can I better imitate Christ's meekness and humility?

5. Reflect on your own strengths and weaknesses. Ask God how He would like to use each to build up the Kingdom of God.

Prayer

Loving God, help me today to be truly humble. Help me to be gentle and loving, to put others ahead of myself, and to put You above all things. Amen.

CHAPTER SIX

HONESTY

The honesty of the upright guides them;
the faithless are ruined by their duplicity.

The honest man's virtue makes his way straight,
but by his wickedness the wicked man falls.
Proverbs 11:3, 5

What I'm about to say may cause you to put this book down and never pick it up again. I know what I'm about to do is fraught with peril. You may be so offended that you may never want to have anything to do with me again. If that happens, I understand. It won't be the first time, and probably not the last. I have offended many with one small sentence, to the point where some have walked out of the room as I was giving a talk. But I am called to proclaim the truth in love. So, here we go.

You're a liar.

There, I've said it. And you're still reading. That's a good sign. I'm going to continue to play this dangerous game and ask you to read that sentence again. Maybe even two or three times. Take a moment to reflect on it; let it sink in.

How does that make you feel? I've found there are generally two reactions to that revelation. The first is anger. The gut reaction is, "How dare you say that to me?! Why, I'm an honest person. I don't lie!" Believe me, I understand that reaction. After all, is there anything more demeaning you can call someone? No one wants to be thought of as a liar. We like to think we are people of our word. Liar is a label nobody wants.

The second reaction, and the one I'm shooting for, is resignation. If we can get through the defiance and the embarrassment, we will come to the stark realization that that statement is, indeed, true. I am a liar.

Remember in the chapter on humility, where one of the attributes of the humble person is knowing they have strengths and weaknesses? Well, my friend, this is one of our weaknesses. For many of us, it is (or, hopefully, was) a habit. I say this by way of experience. You see, I grew up in a household where alcoholism was present. As the child of an alcoholic, I learned to lie. There were certain things you didn't talk about, so you covered them up with lies. In time, it becomes the norm; it actually becomes second nature. I'm not trying to make excuses or brush off sinful behavior. I am responsible for everything that comes out of my mouth. I'm simply sharing a life experience that may help explain how it got started in the first place. Most all households where there is dysfunction (alcoholism, drug abuse, abusive behavior, etc.) are breeding grounds for habitual lying.

Maybe you didn't grow up in a dysfunctional household. That's great! But you still learned to lie at an early age. When kids do something wrong, they lie to try to cover their tracks. It's in our nature. You know, that whole Adam and Eve thing. Every time they get away with a lie, they see it as an effective strategy for getting or doing what they want, and every time they get caught, they try to think of more effective ways to get over on Mom and Dad. You did it, I did it, we all did it. And, like it or not, we all do it still.

It's What Comes Out That Matters

When I was in the early stages of my conversion process, there was a Scripture passage that hit me over the head like a Louisville Slugger when it came to this particular malady.

He summoned the crowd and said to them,
"Hear and understand.
It is not what enters one's mouth that defiles that person;
but what comes out of the mouth is what defiles one.
The things that come out of the mouth come from the heart,
and they defile. For from the heart come evil thoughts,
murder, adultery, unchastity, theft, false witness, blasphemy.
These are what defile a person."
Matthew 15:10-11, 18-20

Those words stung me to the core. I came to the stark realization that when I lied, when I cursed, when I spoke hurtful words, when I objectified other people, these were all offensive to God. To be honest, I had never really considered that before. For you, that may be a no-brainer. But understand that I was in a very different place than I am today. Many, many people are in that same place where I was. They don't understand that what comes out of our mouth can defile us, can be offensive to God. This is why the Magnetic Christian must set an example.

The Jews thought eating certain foods would defile them, or make them unclean. Does it seem that there is a similar attitude in our culture today? By that I mean so many people are so conscious about their weight and their appearance, they almost think it is a sin to eat certain foods. (Isn't it ironic that obesity is at epidemic levels?) Being healthy is a great thing, and we should be judicious about what we put into our mouths. But how much different would things be if we were so ultra-conscious about that which comes out of our mouths?

In overcoming addiction, the first step to healing is admitting there is a problem. When it comes to lying, this may be the most difficult of all exercises for the disciple. For some this notion of being a liar is easy to admit. For others, it may take a bit of drilling down to the core. It is not until we do this drilling down that we can come to the honest conclusion, and then begin to rectify the problem. Take this to prayer and ask God to reveal to you the ways you are untruthful, to others, to yourself, and even to God.

Why We Lie
Take a look at some of the reasons why we lie. I think one of the most common reasons is to impress other people. We inflate ourselves so others will think well of us. Someone may ask, "Hey, did you hear about such and such?" Our

ready response is, "Yeah, isn't that wild," when in truth we have no idea what they are talking about. Why? Because we don't want to appear stupid or uninformed. We want to be seen as in the know. This is sad, really, because we are missing an opportunity to gain information or knowledge. But our ego tells us that if we reply in the negative, we will be looked down upon, out of touch. The Magnetic Christian knows how to turn this into a positive. Acknowledge that you don't know, then begin asking questions. (See the chapter on Friendliness and listening skills.) Rather than making your-self look dumb, you begin to make the person to whom you are speaking feel good. They have imparted knowledge and information. You have al-lowed them to help you. Just about everyone wants to be thought of as helpful.

> **MAGNETIC INSIGHT:**
> *Honesty must begin within our own hearts. Only when we face the truth about ourselves can we begin to speak the truth to others.*

"The person who is trustworthy in very small matters is also trustworthy in great ones; and the person who is dishonest in very small matters is also dishonest in great ones."
Luke 16:10

We often lie to try and hide our weaknesses. This can manifest itself in many areas of our lives – mental, physical, spiritual. I think this happens often in the realm of sports. An athlete may be injured, but would never admit it, because that would be perceived as weakness. So he lies about it and the injury gets worse until it becomes career-threatening. A woman may be struggling with depression but tells her friends and co-workers everything is fine. She doesn't want to be considered a complainer or weakling. A man may lie to his wife or his doctor about having chest pains. He justifies it by thinking everything will be fine or that he doesn't want anyone to worry needlessly. After all, he is a tough guy. Of course, when the lie is found out, it causes pain, mistrust and heartache.

Another reason we lie is to avoid responsibility. This starts early in life and easily becomes a habit. My parents had six kids in eight years. When Mom would yell, "Who left these dirty dishes here?" the response would come from every corner of the house, "Not me!" No one wanted to take responsibility and have to wash the dishes. Besides, one of my brothers or sisters probably left a dish there too, so it's not my fault. Since everyone else did it, I don't need to come clean. Childish? You bet. That same kind of attitude is so prevalent in the world today in the form of the victim mentality. Everything is someone else's fault. I don't have to take responsibility because I didn't do anything wrong! And besides, everyone is doing it, so it must be okay. This is a big lie that is being encouraged today. The Magnetic Christian must avoid this at all cost. Honesty must begin within our own hearts. Only when we face the truth about ourselves can we begin to speak the truth to others.

Therefore, putting away falsehood, speak the truth, each one to his neighbor, for we are members one of another.
Ephesians 4:25

"Christian" Lies

There is an alarming trend in Christianity today that flies in the face of honesty: the prosperity gospel. The preachers of the prosperity gospel will tell people that if they make a donation to their ministry, God will multiply that donation thirty or sixty or a hundredfold and all their worries - financial, physical, emotional, spiritual - will disappear. Of course, the bigger the donation, the bigger the blessing that will be returned to the faithful. You'll be able to get that new house, that nice Mercedes, the designer clothes, etc. Just give all your money to me and all your troubles will be a thing of the past! It's an attractive message. It's also a lie straight from the mouth of the devil.

MAGNETIC INSIGHT: *When the Magnetic Christian encourages someone to walk with Christ, they must let them know that the cost will be high, indeed. In fact, it will be everything.*

I recently experienced this first hand in a way that initially turned my stomach, then made me want to cry, then got me infuriated. I was staying in a hotel for a conference at which I was speaking. I generally get up very early in the morning. Having a few hours to kill, I flipped on the TV to catch some local weather and news. While channel surfing, I came across a Christian TV network. They were broadcasting a service from what appeared to be a fairly small church. The guy on stage was preaching the full-on prosperity gospel. What really struck me, though, was when he told his followers (and viewers) to bow their heads and join him in a prayer. He squinted his eyes closed and prayed, "Lord, we want more stuff! Lord, we want more stuff! Lord, we want more stuff!" I almost threw up. Friend, if a preacher is telling you that God wants you to have more stuff, I suggest you turn and run in the opposite direction as fast as your legs will carry you – and tell everyone around you to do the same.

Interestingly, the prosperity gospel preachers generally tend to have nice homes, drive nice cars, wear designer clothes, etc. Meanwhile, their adherents continue to get poorer. It reminds me of this old scam: Put an ad in the paper that says, "Send me $20 and I'll tell you how to get rich!" When the unsuspecting rube sends their $20, they receive back a two cent piece of paper that says: Put an ad in the paper telling people to send you $20 and you'll tell them how to get rich!

Telling the Truth

I don't recall one single instance of Jesus asking for money or stuff. If my reading of the Gospels is correct, Jesus was homeless and poor. He had zero possessions. Christ told his disciples again and again that they must take up their cross and follow Him. The Christian road is not an easy road. The Magnetic Christian must be honest about this. How, then, do we balance this hard message with the first attribute of positivity? It can sometimes seem to be a tenuous relationship. In reality, it is not hard at all.

In business, as in most all areas of life, before making a decision, one has to do a cost/benefit analysis. You must figure out what something is going to cost, and what benefits will be derived from that expenditure. If the benefits outweigh the cost, then you're generally making a good decision. When the Magnetic Christian encourages someone to walk with Christ, they must let them know that the cost will be high indeed. In fact, it will be everything. One could then rightly ask, "How can you come up with enough benefits that could possibly outweigh that?"

The answer is simple: eternal life. Heaven. Eternal joy with God. I don't care how long you're going to be walking around on the planet, eternity is going to be a lot longer than that. It's a pretty convincing selling point, if you ask me! But what about the here and now? Are there any earthly benefits to the whole "take up your cross" thing? Absolutely! St. Paul describes some of them in his Letter to the Galatians.

The fruit of the Spirit is love, joy, peace, patience, kindness, generosity, faithfulness, gentleness, self-control.
Galatians 5:22-23

Let me ask you, could you use an extra dose of any of those things? I know I sure can! This is a truth we can honestly share with anyone and everyone!

The Truth is a Person
Of course, the ultimate example of honesty is Jesus. He not only spoke the truth, He IS the Truth! There is a very interesting example of Jesus' honesty in Luke 11. Jesus is invited to dine at the home of a Pharisee. While there, Jesus begins to denounce the Pharisees. He pronounces many "woes" on them. Upon hearing this, a scholar of the law ap-

proaches Jesus and says, "Teacher, by saying this you are insulting us, too." Instead of apologizing and backing off of what He had just said for fear of ruffling feathers or offending anyone, Jesus goes off on the scholars of the law, too. He told them the truth about what they were doing. He had to. They needed to hear the truth so they could have the opportunity to repent. In recounting this story, I'm not suggesting that we run all over the place telling people their sins. That would most probably be counter-productive. We must speak the truth. But the WAY we speak the truth is of paramount importance. We must always speak the truth in love.

Let's be honest. (A good thing, given the chapter we're in!) This is not always going to be easy. Being honest and speaking the truth, especially in a public setting, is going to ruffle some feathers. In our day and age, political correctness frowns on honesty, on speaking the truth. But when we see injustices in the world, when we see people that are doing wrong, that are leading others astray, it is incumbent upon us to be honest and boldly speak the truth. It will, at times, be costly. But we must always remember the reward.

People want to be told the truth, straight up. There is no need to water down or sugarcoat the Gospel. When someone feels (or knows) they are being lied to, it can cause irreparable harm. Rather than attracting people to Christ, it will invariably push them away. How often have you heard people refer to Christians as hypocrites? What is hypocrisy if not lying? Lying damages the one telling the lie, the one receiving the lie, and the relationship of both with God. Abraham

Lincoln once said, "Honesty is the best policy." For the Magnetic Christian, it is the only policy.

Stop lying to one another, since you have taken off the old self with its practices and have put on the new self, which is being renewed, for knowledge, in the image of its creator.
Colossians 3:9-10

Questions for Reflection
1. What do I lie about? (Remember, the chapter is about honesty!)

2. How can I become more transparent?

3. Am I willing to be honest and stand up for the truth?

4. Have I damaged relationships in the past because of lying? Ask God for forgiveness.

5. Are there things in my past that caused me to lie that need healing? Invite God into that area and allow Him to heal you today.

Prayer
Father, forgive me for the many lies that I have told in my life. Help me to always be truthful and honest with you, myself and others. May I always speak the truth in love. Amen.

CHAPTER SEVEN

KINDNESS

Your kindness should be known to all. The Lord is near.
Philippians 4:5

A woman and her three rambunctious children were checking out at the grocery store. The cart was about three-quarters full, leaving just enough room for the smallest child, who was inside the cart gleefully throwing the items onto the conveyor belt. After all the scanning and beeping, the woman pulled out her purse and removed a handful of coupons. When all the additions and subtractions were complete, she pulled out a small wad of cash. Too small, as it turned out. Embarrassed, the woman told the clerk that she was four dollars short. Could she please return some of the items, she asked. All the while, another woman was patiently waiting next in line. When she saw the mother's dilemma, she pulled out her purse and handed the cashier a five dollar bill. "No need to return anything," she said, "I'll take care of it." The young mother thanked her profusely, promising to return the favor someday.

A random act of kindness.

Kindness, like many of the attributes of the Magnetic Christian, is closely linked with other attributes. And, like the Magnetic Christian, kindness is rooted in love. Jesus gives us a glimpse into what constitutes kindness in the Sermon on the Plain from Luke 6. He also affirms what is revealed throughout Scripture, that kindness is an attribute of God Himself.

"Give to everyone who asks of you, and from the one who takes what is yours do not demand it back. Do to others as you would have them do to you. For if you love those who love you, what credit is that to you? Even sinners love those who love them. And if you do good to those who do good to you, what credit is that to you? Even sinners do the same. If you lend money to those from whom you expect repayment, what credit [is] that to you? Even sinners lend to sinners, and get back the same amount. But rather, love your enemies and do good to them, and lend expecting nothing back; then your reward will be great and you will be children of the Most High, for he himself is kind to the ungrateful and the wicked."
Luke 6:30-35

I think it is important to notice in our example from the grocery store that the woman who showed kindness had no idea what the other woman was like. This is what truly makes it kindness. The mother of three could have been the meanest, nastiest woman ever. Or she could have been the nicest, most generous woman ever. The key is that it didn't matter. The woman who showed kindness did it because it was in her heart. It was part of who she was. The mother may not have "deserved" kindness at all. So it is with us and God. We do not deserve one drop of God's kindness. Yet he lavishes it upon us, not because of what we are or what we do, but because

> **MAGNETIC INSIGHT:**
> *You can try to pull the wool over people's eyes, and at times you may be successful. But you can never fool God.*
> *He knows your heart.*

of who He is. And so it is with the Magnetic Christian. We show kindness because we wish to imitate God. King David sang over and over again about the kindness of God.

> *Your deed I did not hide within my heart;*
> *your loyal deliverance I have proclaimed.*
> *I made no secret of your enduring kindness*
> *to a great assembly.*

> *LORD, do not withhold your compassion from me;*
> *may your enduring kindness ever preserve me.*

Psalm 40:11-12

Motivation

So kindness is the Spirit working within us that compels us to do nice things for others – gratuitously, sometimes even undeservedly. It is the living out of the Golden Rule. Kindness, like love, seeks nothing for the self. If an act of kindness is done for something in return, then it probably isn't really an act of kindness at all. Kindness has no ulterior motive. Its only motive is to benefit another.

Ah, motive. Now would be a good time to talk about motive, about what motivates us. As with so much of the Christian life, motive is of the utmost importance. The funny thing about motive is that you're the only one who really knows what your motive is in any given instance. Your motivation for doing something is most often known only to you...and God. This is key for the Magnetic Christian. God always knows what your motive is. You can try to pull the wool over people's eyes, and at times you may be successful. You may even fool yourself at times. (Remember the chapter about Honesty.) But you can never fool God. He knows your heart. He knows what the motivation is behind your every deed.

We must always be careful about attributing motives to the actions of others. We can never really know what is in someone's heart unless they tell us. As Magnetic Christians, we should always try to give others the benefit of the doubt when it comes to motive. Be prudent, but assume their motives are good unless you know otherwise. That being said, sometimes we are able to sniff out insincere motives. Like the salesman who wants to upsell us, not because the higher priced product is what we truly need, but because it will increase his commission. Or the guy who buys dinner and drinks for a woman, hoping that she will end up in his bed that night. If we are expecting anything in return, it greatly diminishes the act of kindness, if it is even kindness at all. The recipient of the kindness may not be aware of the ulterior motive. This makes it even more sinister. This kind of behavior must not be a part of the Magnetic Christian's life.

A Matter of the Heart

Jesus spent his life showing kindness. Feeding the multitudes, healing the sick, casting out demons, preaching and teaching; His motivation was always the good of the people. We hear this from the mouth of the Lord himself in the story of the feeding of the four thousand.

In those days when there again was a great crowd without anything to eat, he summoned the disciples and said, "My heart is moved with pity for the crowd, because they have been with me now for three days and have nothing to eat. If I send them away hungry to their homes, they will collapse on the way, and some of them have come a great distance."
Mark 8:1-3

Jesus' motivation was not to gain accolades or be rewarded in any way. His heart was moved. He was filled with love, and put His love into action, expecting nothing in return. As imitators of Christ, this must always be our motivation for showing kindness. We must remember, too, that kindness most often has nothing to do with the material. Oh, we may be part of the meal chain for a family who has lost a loved one or has a child in the hospital. We may plunk a five dollar bill in the hand of the homeless guy at the end of the exit ramp. These things are certainly kind and holy. But often the most valuable act of kindness we can do has nothing to do with meeting the material needs of another. They have everything to do with meeting a much deeper spiritual need – the desire to be noticed, to be accepted. A kind word. Greeting a stranger with a smile. A gentle hug. A word of encouragement. Opening a door for an elderly person. These things are often far more valuable than any amount of money or material goods. Ask God to show you throughout the day how you can show kindness to others.

Kindness and Mercy

In our church, we sing a beautiful hymn based on Psalm 103:8, which says, "Merciful and gracious is the Lord, slow to anger, abounding in kindness." It speaks of God's kindness and mercy. Honestly, I tear up every time we sing it. Why does this song affect me so deeply? Because I know the Lord has been kind and merciful to me. If you think about it, kindness and mercy are so closely related that you really can't tell them apart. Every act of mercy is really an act of kindness, and every act of kindness certainly has an element of mercy in it. To show kindness is to show mercy, and to show mercy is to show kindness. To show either is to imitate Christ.

> **MAGNETIC INSIGHT:**
> *Thanks be to God that His kindness and mercy are not dependent upon whether or not we are deserving. So it should be with our kindness and mercy.*

Recall the woman in the grocery store. As we said, she may not have "deserved" that act of kindness. The same is true of mercy. We don't deserve one iota of God's mercy. But that doesn't stop God from being merciful. Why? Because it is part of God's makeup. Is it also a part of our makeup? If we wish to be Magnetic Christians, it must be. Consider this story from John's Gospel.

*Early in the morning he arrived again in the temple area,
and all the people started coming to him, and he sat down
and taught them. Then the scribes and Pharisees brought
a woman who had been caught in adultery and made her
stand in the middle. They said to him, "Teacher, this woman
was caught in the very act of committing adultery. Now in
the law, Moses commanded us to stone such women. So
what do you say?" They said this to test him, so that they
could have some charge to bring against him. Jesus bent
down and began to write on the ground with his finger. But
when they continued asking him, he straightened up and
said to them, "Let the one among you who is without sin be
the first to throw a stone at her." Again he bent down and
wrote on the ground. And in response, they went away one
by one, beginning with the elders. So he was left alone with
the woman before him. Then Jesus straightened up and said
to her, "Woman, where are they? Has no one condemned
you?" She replied, "No one, sir." Then Jesus said,
"Neither do I condemn you.
Go, [and] from now on do not sin any more."*
John 8:2-11

Talk about kindness and mercy! This woman's fate was
in Jesus' hands. Had Jesus said, "Yes, you must follow the
law of Moses," the woman would have surely been stoned
to death. We must realize that, according to the law, ston-
ing is what she deserved. Yet Jesus showed her mercy. His
kindness and mercy were completely undeserved. She was

guilty, guilty, guilty – as are we.

Imagine what our lives would be like if God only showed us kindness and mercy when we deserved it. I daresay that He would never show us kindness and mercy! But thanks be to God that His kindness and mercy are not dependent upon whether or not we are deserving. So it should be with our kindness and mercy.

I want to make one more point about the story of the woman caught in adultery. While Jesus showed her kindness and mercy, please notice that He did not approve of or condone her actions. In fact, He reminded her that what she had done was sinful, and that she should not sin any more. I bring this up because so many people today engage in moral relativism. They try to say that right and wrong are whatever any individual says is right and wrong. They claim that there are no moral absolutes, no rules of morality that govern all people. They want to try to justify their own sinful behavior, and often they break out this passage of Scripture. "Let he who is without sin cast the first stone," they cry. "You can't tell me that I'm sinning!"

Take another look at the example of Jesus. Saving the woman's life was certainly an act of kindness and mercy. But perhaps an even greater act of kindness was to help the woman with her spiritual malady: sin. By reminding her of the fact that her actions were sinful, i.e. leading her away from God, Jesus showed that He was even more concerned about her soul. I don't point this out to say we have license to go around pointing out everyone's sins to them. I believe most people know that they are sinning. God's laws are written on our hearts. Sometimes a gentle reminder is just what someone needs to begin the process of setting things right with God. Be very careful with this, though! I don't think anyone has ever been badgered into the Kingdom of God. Quite the contrary; most people will just dig in their heels when they feel that they are being pushed too hard or against their will. As much as we desire to see someone, especially our loved ones, get right with God, there can be a fine line between drawing them closer and pushing them away. Nagging and finger wagging will almost certainly push them away, even if our intentions are good. Follow the Holy Spirit's leadings on that one.

Coming Around to Home

A final note about kindness, and one that I hope will cause reflection and self-examination. I have found that for many, it is easy to show kindness to strangers. Yet we often neglect to do so for those we love the most, those closest to us. You have probably experienced this. In fact, you may be guilty of it yourself.

We probably all know someone like this; they may even live in our own house. The man who volunteers for every charitable organization at the church. He spends many nights at meetings and goes out on weekends, cooking at the church picnic, feeding the poor, greeting people as they enter the church. He would give a total stranger the shirt off his back. "What a kind soul!" people say about him. Yet when he gets home, he never has a kind word for his wife. She can't remember the last time he took her to dinner, bought her flowers or complimented her. He neglects and/or criticizes his children incessantly. Or, worse yet, ignores them.

The woman who always has a nice smile for her co-workers. She never turns down an opportunity to help out at the kids' school. Everyone speaks so highly of her. "Supermom!" they call her. But she never ceases nagging her children about their grades, not cleaning their rooms, not sitting up straight in church, etc., etc. Her kids feel as though they can't do anything right.

Now, I'm not trying to lay a guilt trip on anyone. But I can tell you that the old axiom, "Charity begins at home," is often neglected if not forgotten. Kindness is not something we reserve for strangers or friends. The ones we most need to show kindness to are those that we love the most. St. Paul spoke of this principle.

So then, while we have the opportunity, let us do good
to all, but especially to those who belong to
the family of the faith.
Galatians 6:10

That "family of the faith" must first be our own family. The Magnetic Christian leads by example, showing love, respect and kindness to those they love the most. I'll end by sharing a couple of things that have been a blessing to my family. Many years ago Zig Ziglar told the story of how he always opens the car door for his wife whenever she gets in or out of the car. I adopted that practice because I believe it is important to make my bride feel special. That small act of kindness is one that often gets comments from others. Men, I recommend it highly. Show the world that chivalry is not dead! The other thing I do is something that I just did with you. Whenever I refer to my wife, Michelle, in public, I call her my bride. You wouldn't believe how many emails I get, mostly from women, who think that is so special – and they're right; I do it because my bride is special, and I always want her to feel that way.

Always remember: Kindness is contagious. Spread some around today.

Questions for Reflection

1. Would I consider myself a kind person? If so, why? If not, why not?

2. How has the Lord been kind to me? Reflect on some of your blessings.

3. Are my kind deeds ever done with ulterior motives? What are they and why? Ask God to cleanse your heart of those.

4. What are some ways that I show kindness to those closest to me?

5. What are two things I can do this week to show kindness to my family?

Prayer

Father, I thank you for your great kindness to me, your unworthy servant. Help me today to imitate Jesus and show kindness to all. Amen.

CHAPTER EIGHT

COMPASSION

[And] be kind to one another, compassionate,
forgiving one another as God has forgiven you in Christ.
Ephesians 4:32

A family had an elderly couple that lived a few doors down. The old man was known as the neighborhood curmudgeon. He was always cantankerous and surly. No one dared go near him for fear of getting chewed out. It came to pass that the old man's wife died. A few days after the funeral, the mother of the family went out to the front yard and noticed her six year-old son sitting on the porch swing with the old man. Surprised, she waited until the boy returned home and asked him what they talked about. "Oh," said the boy, "We didn't talk about anything, Mama. I just helped him cry."

Compassion simply means to share in another's passion. It is the ability to "feel" another's suffering. Perhaps you have said to someone before, "I feel for you," or "I feel your pain." That is compassion. It often helps when you have been through a similar experience, but that is not a prerequisite for having compassion. Compassion comes from a heart of love. It is the attribute that enables us to "enter into" another's pain, and to experience that pain with them.

In a sense, compassion causes pain within our own hearts. It is what causes our hearts to ache for another who is suffering. Scientists have found an interesting link between many identical twins. No matter the distance between the two, when one feels pain or hurt, the other senses it, too. This phenomenon is not unlike compassion. When someone else is hurting, we hurt, too. And just like when we hurt and want to alleviate our own pain, compassion causes us to want to help end the suffering of another.

I believe that compassion is an ever-changing, ever-growing attribute. I have certainly found this to be the case in my life. When I was young and inexperienced, I did not have a lot of compassion for others. I don't say this to belittle myself or beat myself up, it is simply a fact. I considered myself to be a tough, self-sufficient, rugged individual. I didn't need anybody to "feel sorry" for me. Thus, I didn't feel the need to feel sorry for anybody else. Truth be told, I didn't see the need to feel much of anything for anybody else. I think this is often the case with a lot of men. We are taught to suppress our feelings. For me, this resulted in a lack of compassion.

All Things Work for Good

I have noticed that as I have gotten older and been through more life experiences, my compassion has risen in kind. I'll give you an example. My father passed away three years ago. He died suddenly of a heart attack. He was alone, no one around to comfort him in his last moments. Before that happened, a number of my friends had lost one or both of their parents, and I had spoken with hundreds of other people who experienced the loss of a parent. I was always sad for them. But I never really knew what they were going through, because I had not gone through it myself. Since the death of my father, my compassion has grown immeasurably for those who have lost loved ones. Having been down that road, I really do "feel" their pain. But that's not all. The Lord has also increased my compassion in most every other situation.

This principle reminds me of something St. Paul wrote to the believers in Rome.

> **MAGNETIC INSIGHT:**
> *It is certainly a good thing to "feel" compassion for another. But like faith, a feeling not put into action is of little value.*

We know that all things work for good for those who love God, who are called according to his purpose.
Romans 8:28

You see, my father's death could have left me bitter and angry. Because of the suddenness of his death, there were issues that Dad and I never really got resolved. It would have been easy to say that he died too young; that God took him too soon. This kind of loss often causes people to become angry with God. We've all seen it happen before. A tragedy befalls someone and they turn their anger toward God. They may even walk away from their faith. Perhaps this has happened to you. Maybe you're even in that place right now. If so, know that it's okay. God gets it. He understands, and He has compassion. As a matter of fact, if you allow it, God will use this to help you grow in your compassion. That is certainly what happened to me. One of the purposes for my dad's death was to help me grow in compassion. So while it was tragic and sad, God used it for good.

Compassion, like all the other attributes of the Magnetic Christian, is not necessarily in and of itself an action. But our compassion must spur us on to action. How can this be manifested in our lives? Let's use God as our example. We know that God is compassionate. The Scriptures are filled with references to this attribute of God.

The LORD is good to all,
compassionate to every creature.
Psalm 145:9

Compassionate and merciful is the LORD;
he forgives sins, he saves in time of trouble.
Sirach 2:11

How do we know that God, or for that matter another person, is compassionate? By their actions. It is certainly a good thing to "feel" compassion for another. But like faith, a feeling not put into action is of little value. So what are some of the things that God does to show His compassion? For starters, God forgives. Forgiveness is truly compassion

96

in action.

The Act of Forgiveness

We must always remember that forgiveness is an act of the will. While on one level compassion is a "feeling," forgiveness is not. Forgiveness is a conscious choice we must make. When we choose to forgive someone, we may not feel it at all. Quite the contrary. We may still harbor feelings of bitterness and anger over the hurt that was perpetrated on us. Yet we must still forgive. Often we must make the choice to do this over and over again for the same offense. Compassion enters in when we realize that we, too, have injured others and need to be forgiven - and so our compassion compels us to forgive those who have wounded us. Once again, it is the living out of the Golden Rule.

While forgiveness is a choice, a decision we must make, it is not an optional one for the Magnetic Christian. Jesus made this abundantly clear in a conversation He had with Peter.

Then Peter approaching asked him, "Lord, if my brother sins against me, how often must I forgive him? As many as seven times?" Jesus answered, "I say to you, not seven times but seventy-seven times. That is why the kingdom of heaven may be likened to a king who decided to settle accounts with his servants. When he began the accounting, a debtor was brought before him who owed him a huge amount. Since he had no way of paying it back, his master ordered him to be sold, along with his wife, his children, and all of his property, in payment of the debt. At that, the

servant fell down, did him homage, and said, 'Be patient with me, and I will pay you back in full.' Moved with compassion the master of that servant let him go and forgave him the loan. When that servant had left, he found one of his fellow servants who owed him a much smaller amount. He seized him and started to choke him, demanding, 'Pay back what you owe.' Falling to his knees, his fellow servant begged him, 'Be patient with me, and I will pay you back.' But he refused. Instead, he had him put in prison until he paid back the debt. Now when his fellow servants saw what had happened, they were deeply disturbed, and went to their master and reported the whole affair. His master summoned him and said to him, 'You wicked servant! I forgave you your entire debt because you begged me to. Should you not have had pity on your fellow servant, as I had pity on you?' Then in anger his master handed him over to the torturer until he should pay back the whole debt.
So will my heavenly Father do to you, unless each of you forgives his brother from his heart."
Matthew 18:21-35

Again, forgiveness is not optional. God knows that it is not easy. It may be the hardest thing you ever do. You may have to forgive over and over and over again for the same offense. You make the decision to forgive and, lo and behold, a wave of bitterness and unforgiveness washes over you. Decide again to forgive – and again and again.

When we make the decision to withhold our forgiveness, when we decide to bear a grudge and hang on to resentment, we do nothing more than imprison ourselves. We chain ourselves into a dark dungeon where little or no light shines. Unforgiveness causes the light of Christ in us to become dim. It is next to impossible for the person who bears grudges, is resentful and hurt and angry all the time to be a Magnetic Christian.

MAGNETIC INSIGHT: *Sometimes prayer is the ONLY thing that we can do for someone. If all you have to offer someone as an act of compassion is prayer, know that you are offering something of the highest order.*

tian. Unforgiveness will mute all of the other attributes of the Magnetic Christian. This is why compassion is so important. When we can relate to another's pain, to their brokenness and wounds, we begin to have a greater understanding of what may have caused them to hurt us in the first place. Compassion breeds forgiveness. Notice in the story from Matthew 18 that the master forgave his servant because he was "moved with compassion." So must we be.

While forgiving someone who has hurt us is often very difficult, I believe there is one person on the planet who many think it is impossible to forgive: themselves. I don't know about you, but I have always been pretty hard on myself. I generally tend to expect a lot from others, and even more from myself. When I mess up, I tend to mess up real good, and it has taken me some real work to learn to forgive myself. Perhaps you have struggled with this. Maybe you're even struggling with it now. If so, I'd like to share a personal experience that really helped me.

Many years ago I was on a silent retreat. I talked with my spiritual director about how hard I was on myself and how I had a difficult time forgiving myself for things I had done. He asked me to do a brief spiritual exercise. Picture yourself sitting in a chair, with Jesus sitting next to you. Now talk to yourself as you normally would, with harsh tones and words of condemnation. "How could you be so stupid? You're such an idiot! You can't do anything right!" How would Jesus react to hearing that? Would Jesus ever speak to you in that way? Of course not! Jesus would speak words of love and peace and forgiveness. Are you not called to imitate Christ? Then do so for yourself! This little exercise worked wonders for me. Try it yourself if you struggle with not being able to forgive yourself. Be like Jesus. He forgives you. So you should forgive you.

Compassion in Action

We show our compassion through acts of kindness and service. We donate to charities, adopt children from foreign lands and volunteer for ministries and non-profit organizations of all sorts. Sometimes our acts of compassion can seem small to us or to others, but they are highly significant to the recipient, as in the story at the beginning of this chapter. St. Paul gives great advice in how to show compassion.

Rejoice with those who rejoice, weep with those who weep.
Romans 12:15

One of the greatest ways of putting our compassion into action is through prayer. I am almost ashamed to admit it, but I didn't always view prayer this way. Like many, I have always been a doer. Sound familiar? I always thought that when it came to doing things, especially things for the Lord, more was better. What good would it be to sit around praying for someone when you could be out raising money, putting on a golf tournament, starting a clothing drive, and on and on and on? It didn't really occur to me that pouring my heart out to God, standing in the gap and asking for a blessing or a healing for someone could be the highest good I could do for them. How wrong I was. In fact, sometimes prayer is the ONLY thing we can do for someone. It never struck me that prayer is actually DOING something! If all you have to offer someone as an act of compassion is a prayer, know that you are offering something of the highest order. Never feel as though prayer is not enough. If we have the ability to do more, to meet someone's physical needs, we should; we must. But we should always begin and end with prayer.

As a father has compassion on his children,
so the LORD has compassion on the faithful.
Psalm 103:13

A final thought on compassion – something that I have struggled with in the past and still struggle with to this day. There are two kinds of people I find it hard to find compassion for in my heart: those with whom I disagree and those that I feel have made bad choices or decisions and need to suffer the consequences. I share this to let you know that God continues to work on my heart concerning these things, and I still have a long way to go. Perhaps you share the same struggles. If so, let us pray for one another.

For most of my life, I have been very active in the pro-life movement. I believe with every fiber of my being that abortion is wrong, that it is the taking of an innocent human life. I believe that God alone is the giver and taker of life. There are many in the world who disagree with me on this. There are even Christians who believe that abortion and euthanasia are fine and moral. We will have to agree to disagree on that subject. I will never change my position on these matters. Nor will I ever back down from defending the unborn, at any cost. My struggle comes in dealing with those who hold the opposite view. My nature wants to argue and condemn. Compassion goes out the window.

Here is how I try to rectify the matter. I must understand that people who think differently from me are simply coming from a different place. I must assume they are truly well-intentioned. They probably have different experiences and backgrounds that cause them to think and believe what they do. The Magnetic Christian must always remember that we must have compassion for a person. This does not mean that we need to agree with them or adopt their ideas or beliefs. On the contrary, if we believe that an idea or agenda is unjust or evil, we must fight it tooth and nail. But we must look at every individual person and remember they have hurts and wounds we may never know about or see. This, in and of itself, should stir our compassion.

The same is true for the other category of people – those who have made bad choices and decisions. I am a great believer in personal responsibility. If I mess up, I should suffer the consequences. If I make bad choices, it's on me. Because of that, I always had a tendency to look down on others who made bad decisions and choices. Tough luck! Let them suffer! This whole situation is of their own making anyway! Once again, compassion takes a powder.

What has God shown me on this? For the most part, people are doing the best they can. We're all just trying to get along in life. There are so many factors that influence our every decision. Sometimes we just make bad decisions. We do things that hurt others, or even hurt ourselves. Who am I to judge the reason why someone made a bad decision? This goes back to imputing motives on others. Once again, I have to realize that the bad choices and decisions were probably made because of past or present wounds, weakness or brokenness. I still believe we must all be responsible for our actions, and that actions must have consequences. But as a Magnetic Christian, I understand that I must have compassion for everyone. After all, what if God suspended His compassion for us whenever we screwed up, made bad choices or did things against His will? I'll tell you what if – we would be in a world of hurt.

Put on then, as God's chosen ones, holy and beloved,
heartfelt compassion, kindness, humility, gentleness, and
patience, bearing with one another
and forgiving one another…
Colossians 3:12-13

Questions for Reflection

1. Do I consider myself to be a compassionate person? If not, why?

2. What are some ways that I show compassion?

3. Are there those for whom I have little or no compassion? Who are they and why do I have a hard time being compassionate toward them?

4. How have my own past wounds shaped my sense of compassion?

5. Reflect on God's mercy and compassion towards you. Are there areas of my life where I can be more compassionate toward others?

6. What are two things that I can do this week to put my compassion into action?

Prayer

Father, you are full of compassion for all of your children. When we hurt, you hurt. Help me to be a more compassionate person, that I might imitate you and draw others to Christ. Amen.

CHAPTER NINE

APPROACHABILITY

A slave of the Lord should not quarrel,
but should be gentle with everyone, able to teach,
tolerant, correcting opponents with kindness.
2 Timothy 2:24

I've often talked about how rotten I think it would be to be a big celebrity. Isn't it funny…I think lots of people would sell their souls to be rich and famous. I mean, how cool would it be to go anywhere and have everyone recognize you and fawn over you? My opinion – not very cool at all. In fact, I think it would stink. Can you imagine what it would be like not to be able to even go to the grocery store? Or worse yet, to have to surround yourself with bodyguards? That way, of course, no one could get near you. You would become unapproachable.

When you stop to think about it, you really don't have to become a big celebrity at all to become unapproachable. People from all walks of life do it all the time. We put up walls and use defense mechanisms so no one can get close to us. Why? The reasons are many, of course. Perhaps we think we are too busy and don't want to be inconvenienced with people bothering us. Maybe we've convinced ourselves that we're too shy or bad conversationalists. Perhaps we lack confidence or feel we don't really have anything to offer others. Maybe you keep people at arm's length because you've

> **MAGNETIC INSIGHT:** *Satan knows that if he can get you to keep your focus on negative and bad thoughts, you will be ineffective in your efforts to draw people to Christ. Use the power of God to rid these thoughts from your mind.*

been burned before. It happens to all of us, right? You get hurt in a relationship and you want to make sure you won't be vulnerable to that again. So you become cold, standoffish. For many, this becomes so much a part of their personality that they don't even realize they're doing it. In fact, it feels quite normal. They sometimes wonder why they don't seem to have many friends; why people seem to be uncomfortable around them. Must be their problem, they think.

This happens in any kind of relationship. From the time we're very young, we have conflicts with other people. Kids at school make fun of us. Tell us we're too fat, too thin, too short, too tall, our teeth are crooked, we dress funny – there is no end to the list. Our parents may have said something in anger that hurt us. Maybe a teacher told us that we'll never amount to anything. Unfortunately, we carry these wounds with us, often for the rest of our lives. We replay those negative "tapes" in our heads until they are ingrained in our psyche. If this has been a pattern in your life, please know you can stop this destructive habit and turn things around to-day! First, recognize the fact that you are allowing negative thought patterns to take over. Next, realize these negative thoughts are not from God. Indeed, I believe these negative thoughts that keep rearing their ugly heads are from the devil himself. Satan knows that if he can get you to keep your focus on negative and bad thoughts, you will be ineffective in your efforts to draw people to Christ. Use the power of God to rid these thoughts from your mind. If you need to, say out loud, "Satan, I REFUSE to allow you a place in my head! I am a child of God!" Remember, acknowledgement is the key. Acknowledge that your thoughts have turned negative and then banish them, and the one who put them there, from your mind completely!

Jesus in the Mirror

Many years ago, I fancied myself a singer/songwriter. I have to admit that I wasn't all that good, but at the time I felt God had given me a gift and I needed to use it for His glory. One of the songs I wrote was called "Jesus in the Mirror." I, like so many others, struggled mightily with my self esteem. I had a tendency to identify myself by my accomplishments. Because of this, I never seemed to measure up. There was always someone smarter, faster, handsomer, richer, more well-spoken – you name it. Because I could never seem to make it to the top of the heap, I always felt like I was at the bottom. Has this ever happened to you? Once again, you are not alone.

I was at a very low point when God, through a very wise

spiritual director, revealed to me the truth that my value is not derived from my accomplishments, or lack thereof. My value lies in the fact that I am a son of God! I don't have to DO anything to merit God's love. In fact, there is nothing I can DO to merit God's love. It is freely given. To me, to you, to all of us. This realization caused me to write "Jesus in the Mirror." In the song, I ask the question, "Who do you see when you look in the mirror? Can you possibly see Jesus staring back at you?" For most it is a difficult, if not impossible, proposition. It is so much easier to see Jesus in others than it is to see Him in ourselves. But if you truly believe that you are created in the image and likeness of God, then you should be able to see Christ in you. Yet this is one of the biggest obstacles people face.

I'd like to propose a quick spiritual exercise for you. Go and stand in front of a mirror. As you look at the image staring back at you, ask God to allow you to see that person through His eyes. Then close your eyes and imagine you're looking upon the face of Jesus. Envision Him clearly, focus on His eyes. Notice that His eyes are filled with love as they stare at you. Jesus is literally drinking in your beauty! Now open your eyes again and see the Jesus in you, staring back at you in the mirror.

The reason I bring this up in the chapter on approachability is that the more you can love yourself, the more you can see Jesus in yourself, the more you will be able to see Jesus in others. You'll be absolutely amazed at how other people will be able to detect this, and will literally be drawn to you!

Have you ever met someone you felt attracted to right away? I'm not talking about sexual attraction, but personal attraction. Chances are very good they exhibited many of the attributes we've already talked about in this book. They exuded friendliness, positivity, confidence, enthusiasm, humility and other traits you found attractive. In fact, didn't you feel like you could walk right up to them, strike up a conversation and become their friend? That you could share anything with them, ask them anything? When you did, they welcomed you into their circle with open arms, didn't they?

The Magnetic Christian is approachable. We want people to feel comfortable with us. We want them to feel like they will be welcomed, like they can talk to us without fear of being judged or looked down upon or cast out. As you may have experienced before in your life, many people have a preconceived notion of Christians. They stereotype Christians as being holier-than-thou, snooty and cliquish. Their idea of a Christian goes like this: If you don't look the way we look, think the way we think, dress the way we dress, believe the way we believe, then you can't be part of the club. There's no room at the inn for people like you! The Magnetic Christian must do everything possible to squelch this notion. We must always try to put people at ease, to let them know that they can come to us.

Jesus as our Example

Of course, the model of approachability is Jesus Himself. The Gospels are chock full of instances where people came to Jesus. They brought their sick, they came to be taught, to be healed, to have demons cast out. Now, some may argue that these people all came to Jesus because they wanted something they thought or knew that Jesus could provide for them. The reason they came to Him was because they knew that He would hear them, touch them, heal them, PAY ATTENTION TO THEM! I include that phrase in all caps because I believe that this is what people really want. Though we all have many needs, our chief want in life is for someone to pay attention to us. We want to be noticed, we want to be thought of as valuable, we want to be loved. This is why so many people struggle with one bad relationship after another. They continually look for love and acceptance and when they don't find it, they move on. It's why young people join gangs. They don't feel that anyone cares about them. This is, I believe, a major reason why people leave the Church or walk away from religion altogether. They want to be accepted for who they are. They want to be appreciated, and they're not getting that from Christians. That's why these are perhaps the greatest gifts the Magnetic Christian has to offer – our time and our attention. When people feel comfortable seeking our time and our attention, we can accomplish much for the Kingdom.

They came to Jericho. And as he was leaving Jericho with his disciples and a sizable crowd, Bartimaeus, a blind man, the son of Timaeus, sat by the roadside begging. On hearing that it was Jesus of Nazareth, he began to cry out and say, "Jesus, son of David, have pity on me." And many rebuked him, telling him to be silent. But he kept calling

110

out all the more, "Son of David, have pity on me." Jesus
stopped and said, "Call him." So they called the blind man,
saying to him, "Take courage; get up, he is calling you."
He threw aside his cloak, sprang up, and came to Jesus.
Jesus said to him in reply, "What do you want me to do for
you?" The blind man replied to him, "Master, I want to
see." Jesus told him, "Go your way; your faith has saved
you." Immediately he received his sight
and followed him on the way.
Mark 10:46-52

Bartimaeus was probably a lot like you and me. For
starters, he had a disability. When you think about it, we all
have disabilities. Ours may not be physical disabilities. It
may be something hidden deep within us that no one else
will ever see. We may do a fine job at hiding our disability
from the rest of the world. But we know it is there, always
lurking, holding us back, filling us with doubt. Bartimaeus
probably had no reasonable expectation that he would be
able to have an encounter with Jesus. Remember, Jesus was
quite famous. The crowds following him continued to grow
and grow. Everyone wanted a piece of him. But Bartimaeus
threw caution to the wind. He spoke up, crying out to Jesus.
He was rebuked. The people around Jesus didn't want to let
him near. While this may have discouraged others, it did not
deter Bartimaeus.

Now let's look at Jesus. Think of the burden that Jesus
must have carried at this time. Great crowds followed Him.
People were constantly seeking Him out, probably pawing

111

at Him just to touch Him. Imagine how emotionally draining this must have been on Jesus. He could have ignored
Bartimaeus' pleas. After all, He was on a journey, on a mission. He could have had one of His disciples minister to the
blind man. But Jesus always put people first. No matter how
important His agenda was, He wanted the people to know
that He was approachable. So He called out to Bartimaeus,
and healed him. Even the outcasts of society felt comfortable
coming to Jesus. Why? Because He was approachable and
magnetic, of course!

It Ain't a Popularity Contest

*A Pharisee invited him to dine with him, and he entered the
Pharisee's house and reclined at table. Now there was a
sinful woman in the city who learned that he was at table
in the house of the Pharisee. Bringing an alabaster flask
of ointment, she stood behind him at his feet and began to
bathe his feet with her tears. Then she wiped them with her
hair, kissed them, and anointed them with the ointment.
When the Pharisee who had invited him saw this he said to
himself, "If this man were a prophet, he would know who
and what sort of woman this is who is touching him, that
she is a sinner." Jesus said to him in reply, "Simon, I have
something to say to you." "Tell me, teacher," he said. "Two
people were in debt to a certain creditor; one owed five
hundred days' wages and the other owed fifty. Since they
were unable to repay the debt, he forgave it for both. Which
of them will love him more?" Simon said in reply, "The
one, I suppose, whose larger debt was forgiven." He said to
him, "You have judged rightly.*

*So I tell you, her many sins have been forgiven; hence,
she has shown great love.*

But the one to whom little is forgiven, loves little."
Luke 7:36-43, 47

The sinful woman in the story above was not afraid to
approach Jesus. In turn, Jesus was not afraid to let her approach. As you see from the Pharisee's reaction, this kind of
behavior from Jesus was nothing short of scandalous. Not
only did Jesus allow this woman near Him, He allowed her
to touch Him! No doubt this would cause Simon the Pharisee
to look askance at Jesus. Many others, those of the "righ-
teous class," felt similarly. Jesus became persona non grata
precisely because He was so approachable. The Gospels are
filled with accounts of people from all walks of life coming
to Jesus. A Pharisee named Nicodemus comes to Him in the
dead of night to ask Him questions. Lepers, who knew better than to approach anyone, come to Him individually, in
pairs, even ten at a time. A diminutive tax collector named
Zacchaeus climbs a tree just to catch a glimpse of Him – and
Jesus goes to his house for dinner.

Jesus was very popular. But there were many "important" people with whom Jesus was not popular at all. The
key thing for the Magnetic Christian to remember is that Jesus didn't care one whit about whether He was popular or
not. He didn't give a hoot what anybody thought of Him. It's
a good thing Jesus wasn't a politician. Can you imagine the
conversation?

"Gee, Lord, your approval rating went through the ceiling when you raised Lazarus from the dead. You were up in the high eighties! But I have to tell you, after that little get-together with the tax collectors and prostitutes, your numbers are bottoming out. Maybe another one of those water to wine miracles will bring those numbers back up!"

Being a Magnetic Christian is not a popularity contest. Jesus didn't have time to care about His popularity. I'm convinced that He would be completely unconcerned with how many Facebook friends He has, how many hits are on His web site or any other number for that matter. He was focused on showing people God's love. On letting people know that heaven – eternal life – is there for the taking, and that He is the Way. What other people thought of Him meant zero. So it must be with the Magnetic Christian. Stop putting so much emphasis on what others think. Concern yourself with what God thinks, with doing God's will. I can assure you that when you are a Magnetic Christian, there will be those who do not like you. There will be some, maybe even "friends" of yours who will think less of you because you choose to associate and show love to those of a different social strata, skin color, income level, etc. Oh, well! You just keep concentrating on bringing the message of God's love. From there, everything will work itself out.

MAGNETIC INSIGHT:
Stop putting so much emphasis on what others think. Concern yourself with what God thinks, with doing God's will.

Then children were brought to him that he might lay his hands
on them and pray. The disciples rebuked them,
but Jesus said, "Let the children come to me,
and do not prevent them;
for the Kingdom of heaven belongs to such as these."
Matthew 19:13-14

The blind, the lame, the sick, lepers, sinners, Pharisees, children – Jesus welcomed them all. And He let them all know He was approachable. There was no reason anyone should be afraid to come to Him. In the above passage from Matthew 19, Jesus encourages the children to come to Him. While He may have been speaking of those who were of a young age, in a broader context, He welcomes all of God's children, young and old, rich and poor, sinners and saints. That is what you should do as a Magnetic Christian – let the children come to you!

Give honor to all, love the community,
fear God, honor the king.
1 Peter 2:17

Questions for Reflection

1. Do I have a tendency to keep people at arm's length? If so, why?

2. Do I continue to play negative "tapes" in my head?

3. Am I ready to banish Satan from having a place in my mind?

4. Am I overly concerned with what others think of me?

How have I let this hold me back from being approachable?

5.   Am I willing to make myself available to all of God's children?

Prayer

Father, help me to be approachable. Help me to love others and welcome them, as Jesus welcomed all. Amen.

CHAPTER TEN

GENEROSITY

Consider this: whoever sows sparingly will also reap sparingly, and whoever sows bountifully will also reap bountifully. Each must do as already determined, without sadness or compulsion, for God loves a cheerful giver.

You are being enriched in every way for all generosity, which through us produces thanksgiving to God...
2 Corinthians 9:6-7, 11

When my dad, Phil Lloyd, died in October 2008, he had just enough money in the bank to pay for a very simple cremation. His ashes are interred in a Veteran's cemetery, which cost his family nothing. He didn't leave a big, fat bank account. He had no hefty life insurance policy to cash in. He drove a beat up old Dodge with several hundred thousand miles on it. On a good day, we may have been able to get a couple hundred bucks for it. For all intents and purposes, Dad died a pauper. Leaving behind five surviving children (one of his sons, my brother, Glenn, was murdered in 1992) and a boatload of grandchildren, some may say he was irresponsible. They would be extremely wrong. You see, Dad had no interest in accumulating money and worldly stuff. When he died, he had nothing left to give because he spent his whole life giving. He was one of the most generous people I have ever known.

The Magnetic Christian is generous. In my lifetime, I have been exceptionally blessed to know so many generous people. Some of them have been blessed with much money and wealth. Many others are much like my dad. They are people of simple means. People that, on the surface, don't appear to have much. When it comes to worldly possessions, that may, indeed, be true. But generosity has NOTHING to do with how much money or stuff one has. Generosity is a matter of the heart. Have you ever looked at someone who is poor and thought that perhaps they are poor because of their great generosity?

Like many of the attributes of the Magnetic Christian, generosity may not come naturally to some. I have to admit right up front that this has been the case for me. Even though I grew up with two of the most generous people on the planet, my mom and dad, I have always struggled with generosity. As with any weakness, this is not something I am proud of or like to admit and talk about. It is something I have to work on every day. But if I

> **MAGNETIC INSIGHT:**
> *As we become better at letting go of things, we become more aware that things – money and possessions – can actually be holding us back from drawing closer to God.*

118

am honest, I must admit it has always been difficult for me to be generous. Acknowledging this has caused me to question why. I have had to dig deep to uncover the reason I struggle with generosity.

It's All About Trust

We've all heard stories about misers. Misers are people who hang on to their money and possessions with white knuckles. They have a very hard time letting go of anything. Like the little old lady who collects soap chips and has five million dollars in the bank. Many of the children of the Depression era didn't know where their next meal was coming from, so they learned to hoard things, just in case. Now, I certainly don't consider myself miserly or a hoarder (though my bride may argue that), but if I am honest, these are traps I could easily fall into. But why are people like that? I certainly don't want to oversimplify, because I know there are often deep-rooted issues that can cause disorders. For me, I think I can answer the question with one word: TRUST.

Generous people trust God. They understand that, no matter what happens in life, God is going to take care of them and provide for them. When you have that innate trust in God, you have no need to amass fortunes or accumulate things or hang on to things. It becomes much easier to let them go because you know God will continue to bless you. Jesus spoke about this trust (or lack thereof) in the Sermon on the Mount.

"Therefore I tell you, do not worry about your life, what you will eat [or drink], or about your body, what you will wear. Is not life more than food and the body more than clothing? Look at the birds in the sky; they do not sow or reap, they gather nothing into barns, yet your heavenly Father feeds them. Are not you more important than they? Can any of you by worrying add a single moment to your life-span? Why are you anxious about clothes? Learn from the way the wild flowers grow. They do not work or spin. But I tell you that not even Solomon in all his splendor was clothed like one of them. If God so clothes the grass of the field, which grows today and is thrown into the oven tomorrow, will he not much more provide for you, O you of little faith? So do not worry and say, 'What are we to eat?' or 'What are we to drink?' or 'What are we to wear?' All these things the pagans seek. Your heavenly Father knows that you need them all. But seek first the kingdom [of God] and his righteousness, and all these things will be given you besides."
Matthew 6:25-33

In a previous chapter, we spoke about fear. I believe that fear is the great killer of trust. And when we don't have trust, we will not be generous. Only when we trust God, when we truly believe that God will take care of our every need (NOT our every WANT), only then can we be truly generous. Then it becomes easy to let go of things. As we become better at letting go of things, we become more aware that things – money and possessions – can actually be holding us back from drawing closer to God.

One of Jesus' favorite topics was our relationship with money and things. Much ink has been spilled about this, and I won't go into a lot of detail about the nuts and bolts of this. Suffice it to say that all of the teachings of Jesus on this have a bearing on our sense of generosity. There are dozens of passages in Scripture that make reference to this relationship. Here are just a few for your meditation:

Then he said to the crowd,
"Take care to guard against all greed,
for though one may be rich,
one's life does not consist of possessions."
Luke 12:15

"No one can serve two masters.
He will either hate one and love the other,
or be devoted to one and despise the other.
You cannot serve God and mammon."
Matthew 6:24

Jesus, looking at him, loved him and said to him,
"You are lacking in one thing. Go, sell what you have
and give to [the] poor and you will have treasure
in heaven; then come, follow me."
At that statement his face fell, and he went away sad,
for he had many possessions.
Mark 10:21-22

Then he told them a parable. "There was a rich man
whose land produced a bountiful harvest. He asked him-
self, 'What shall I do, for I do not have space to store my

harvest?' And he said, 'This is what I shall do: I shall tear down my barns and build larger ones. There I shall store all my grain and other goods and I shall say to myself, "Now as for you, you have so many good things stored up for many years, rest, eat, drink, be merry!" ' But God said to him, 'You fool, this night your life will be demanded of you; and the things you have prepared, to whom will they belong?' Thus will it be for the one who stores up treasure for himself but is not rich in what matters to God."

Luke 12:16-21

It's a Gift!

There are many others, and I hope you will take some time to read the Gospels and become ever more aware of Jesus' teachings about how we look at money and possessions. Here's the bottom line for me on this matter: we must always view everything we have as a gift from God. God has given us everything freely, as a gift, and God expects us to share them freely, as a gift. If we think we have gained anything at all by our own power, we are sorely mistaken. We have fallen once again into the sin of pride. Only when we view everything as gift will we realize that nothing is ours to begin with! Everything that we have is simply on loan from God. And all that we have been given is expected to be used in service to the Kingdom of God.

For the Magnetic Christian, generosity is not an optional thing.

"Much will be required of the person entrusted with much,

and still more will be demanded of the person
entrusted with more."
Luke 12:48

It does not matter what you do (or did) for a living. It does not matter how much (or little) you have in the bank. It does not matter what kind of car you drive, clothes you wear, home you live in, where you shop, or anything else for that matter. None of these things should have any bearing on how generous you are. As Magnetic Christians, we must realize that we have been given much, and much is expected of us.

Too many people are under the mistaken impression that generosity is about money. As though how much money you have available to give away amounts to a hill of beans with God. I assure you it doesn't. If you have been blessed with money, then you will be expected to use it for its intended purpose: to build up the Kingdom of God. But the AMOUNT of money means little. There is a wonderful story in the Scriptures that illustrates this point perfectly.

He sat down opposite the treasury and observed how the
crowd put money into the treasury. Many rich people put in
large sums. A poor widow also came and put in two small
coins worth a few cents. Calling his disciples to himself,
he said to them, "Amen, I say to you, this poor widow put
in more than all the other contributors to the treasury. For
they have all contributed from their surplus wealth, but she,
from her poverty, has contributed all she had,
her whole livelihood."
Mark 12:41-44

So wait…these two small coins worth only a couple of cents were greater than the vast amounts that the rich people put in? You betcha! The rich people wouldn't even miss the money they had given. But the widow gave all she had. Why do you think that was? If you answered TRUST, then give yourself a prize! The widow trusted that God would take care of her, even though after giving all she had to help others, she was left with nothing for herself. Nothing, that is, except faith. But that is worth more money than exists in the entire world.

Tithing

While we're on the topic of money, I want to issue you a challenge. The biblical standard of giving is the tithe. This means 10% of your gross income, before Uncle Sam and everyone else have the opportunity to dip into your earnings. The tithe is the benchmark that the Magnetic Christian should shoot for. We see this clearly in the Book of Malachi.

> *Bring the whole tithe into the storehouse,*
> *That there may be food in my house,*
> *and try me in this, says the LORD of hosts:*
> *Shall I not open for you the floodgates of heaven,*
> *to pour down blessing upon you without measure?*
> ***Malachi 3:10***

Be sure and read through that a couple of times. This is a direct challenge from God! He says, "Try me in this!" God is throwing down the gauntlet! For most people, this notion seems almost absurd. Especially in these difficult economic times, even the thought of giving 10% is frightening. I have had a real struggle with this, too. Shoot, there are times when I still don't quite get it. But my wife always reminds me, "You can't out-give God." Remember, it's all His anyway! Doesn't giving back 10% really seem small in comparison to what He's given us?

"For where your treasure is, there also will your heart be."
Luke 12:34

On the whole, Christians are generous people. But when it comes to meeting this standard of the tithe, we fall quite short. Studies show that most Christians give in the area of 2% of their income to charity. Some give more and some give less, but that is close to the average. Where are you on that scale?

MAGNETIC INSIGHT:
Remember, fear is the destroyer of trust.
Fear kills our spirit of generosity.

Here's the challenge: take a close look at where your money goes. In light of Jesus' words from Luke 12:34, you'll find where your heart is. For many, this can be a sobering exercise. You may find you're spending an awful lot on things that aren't building up the Kingdom of God. Figure out the percentage that you are giving to your church and to charity. If you're like most, you'll probably be in that 2% range. Ask God if you can do better. Then make a plan to bump up your charitable giving by 1%. I believe you'll find it easier than it sounds. And I know that God will honor that effort. When you've settled into that, try going up another half or even a full percent. As you go through this, try to be ever more aware of how God is providing for and blessing you and your family. I know you will be amazed by the results. Believe me, if you're like me and struggle with generosity and trusting God, it gets easier, and more fun, with practice!

> *In generous spirit pay homage to the LORD,*
> *be not sparing of freewill gifts.*
> *With each contribution show a cheerful countenance,*
> *and pay your tithes in a spirit of joy.*
> *Give to the Most High as he has given to you,*
> *generously, according to your means.*
> **Sirach 35:7-9**

Time, Talent and Treasure

What this all boils down to is being a good steward of that which God has given you. And remember, God has given you everything. We need to always be aware of how we are "spending" our resources. These are often thought of in terms of time, talent and treasure. Read the following parable and ask yourself how well you are investing your resources in these three areas.

"It will be as when a man who was going on a journey called in his servants and entrusted his possessions to them. To one he gave five talents; to another, two; to a third, one – to each according to his ability. Then he went away. Immediately the one who received five talents went and traded with them and made another five. Likewise, the one who received two made another two. But the man who received

one went off and dug a hole in the ground and buried his master's money. After a long time the master of those servants came back and settled accounts with them. The one who had received five talents came forward bringing the additional five. He said, 'Master, you gave me five talents. See, I have made five more.' His master said to him, 'Well done, my good and faithful servant. Since you were faithful in small matters I will give you great responsibilities. Come, share your master's joy.' [Then] the one who had received two talents also came forward and said, 'Master, you gave me two talents. See, I have made two more.' His master said to him, 'Well done, my good and faithful servant. Since you were faithful in small matters, I will give you great responsibilities. Come, share your master's joy.' Then the one who had received one talent came forward and said, 'Master, I knew you were a demanding person, harvesting where you did not plant and gathering where you did not scatter; so of fear I went off and buried your talent in the ground. Here it is back.' His master said to him in reply, 'You wicked, lazy servant! So you knew that I harvest where I did not plant and gather where I did not scatter? Should you not then have put my money in the bank so that I could have got it back with interest on my return? Now then! Take the talent from him and give it to the one with ten. For to everyone who has, more will be given and he will grow rich; but from the one who has not, even what he has will be taken away. And throw this useless servant into the darkness outside, where there will be wailing and grinding of teeth.'"

Matthew 25:14-30

There are a few key points we need to reflect on in this passage. First, isn't it interesting that the currency is called talents? This should be a reminder that this parable is about much more than money. God expects us to invest our talents (and time and treasure) into building up the Kingdom of God. God expects a return on His investment!

Next, notice what the master gives to the faithful servants who have generously invested that which they had been given to bring a return for the master. He gives them great responsibilities! Many people would probably balk at that. "Hey, I've got enough on my plate, Lord! The last thing I need is more responsibilities!" But look carefully at the very next thing the master says. "Come, share your master's joy!" The Magnetic Christian views serving the Lord and investing all that God has given us as a joy, not drudgery. Generosity brings great joy to our lives, and the lives of others!

This leads us to the attitude of the final servant, the one who did not invest his gift to bring a return to the master. Notice that he says to the master, "Out of fear I went off and buried your talent in the ground." This unfaithful servant acted out of fear and not gratefulness and generosity. Remember, fear is the destroyer of trust. Fear kills our spirit of generosity. In the end, this servant's lack of trust and generosity cost him everything.

Jesus as Our Example

Many people fail to remember that Jesus was a homeless man with no possessions. There is nothing wrong with owning things. The problem comes when we allow things to own us, when we put money and possessions ahead of people, stuff ahead of relationships. If people sense that we care more about material things than about them, they will not be attracted toward us, but repulsed. The more we allow Jesus to take precedence in our lives, the more generous we become.

If we were to include all the passages of Scripture that point to the generosity of Jesus, you would pretty much be holding all four Gospels in your hand. Jesus is the model of generosity. During His time on earth He gave fully of Himself in preaching, teaching, healing, praying, feeding and giving. But for the greatest example of the generosity of Jesus, we need look no further than the cross. Here Jesus gave you His all. He made the ultimate investment in your eternal future. Let us use Christ as our example and through our generosity, bring others to Him.

> *"Without cost you have received;*
> *without cost you are to give."*
> ***Matthew 10:8***

Questions for Reflection

1. Would I consider myself to be a generous person?

2. What are some things that are holding me back from being more generous?

3. How close am I now to meeting the Biblical standard of the tithe (10%)? Am I willing to give more in the coming months?

4. Do I truly trust that God will meet my every need? How can I grow more deeply in trust?

5. Am I a cheerful giver? Do I find great joy in giving of my time, talent and treasure? If not, why not?

6. What steps can I take in the coming weeks and months to be more generous?

Prayer

Father, help me to understand more and more that all that I have is a gift from you. Fill me with gratitude and a generous heart, that others may see your generosity shining out through me. Amen.

CHAPTER ELEVEN

ENCOURAGEMENT

*We must consider how to rouse one another to love and
good works. We should not stay away from our assembly, as
is the custom of some, but encourage one another,
and this all the more as you see the day drawing near.*
Hebrews 10:24-25

I'm a runner. Not a good one, mind you, but I run a lot.
I've done 5Ks, 10Ks, 15Ks, half marathons, marathons
and even an ultra-marathon. Doing all that running re-
quires a lot of training. You don't just lace up your shoes
one day and go run 26.2 miles. It takes a lot of time and
dedication. I've learned a lot about myself in the years that I
have been running. One of the most important things I have
learned is that, even though running may seem to be a soli-
tary sport, there is no way I could have done any of this by
myself.

When I'm in training, I always run with a group. Every
Saturday morning, I crawl out of bed at an ungodly hour
(usually around 4 a.m.) and join up with my running group.
Over the years these guys have become my best friends, my

confidants, my mentors, my advisors, my buddies. Roger, Glenn, Andy, Patrick, James, Jerry, Joe, Ruben, Nick, Bob, Ed, Luis, Carlos and so many others have gotten me through many a mile. We have seen each other through injuries and pain, personal records and bonks, births and deaths, graduations and weddings and everything else that life throws at us. If there is one reason I continue to hang around with these nut jobs, I can sum it up in one word: ENCOURAGEMENT.

I have been exceptionally blessed to have many encouragers in my life. Chief among them are my wife and children and my parents. My wife, Michelle, my four kids and my mom and dad have always been my biggest cheerleaders. Right behind that group are my running buddies. These are the people who are always there

MAGNETIC INSIGHT: *When you help someone pull up that courage from deep within, you will see a change in them that will begin a change in the entire world! This change will ripple through nations and generations.*

challenging, prodding and urging me on when I don't think I can take another step – on the road or in life. They pat me on the back when I've achieved a goal, and comfort me when I've fallen short. They are always ready and willing to lift me up.

> *Therefore, encourage one another and*
> *build one another up, as indeed you do.*
> **1 Thessalonians 5:11**

The Magnetic Christian is an encourager. Encouragement is a natural outgrowth of all the other attributes of the Magnetic Christian. When we practice positivity, enthusiasm, friendliness, confidence, humility, honesty, kindness, compassion, approachability and generosity, a spirit of encouragement will naturally flower within us. But like the other attributes of the Magnetic Christian, encouragement may not come naturally to everyone. For many, it is something that must be worked on. For all, it certainly must be practiced.

The word "encourage" really means "to give courage to." But as Magnetic Christians, we understand that we can't give courage, or any other attribute, to anyone. God has already given these things to His people. He has implanted all these attributes into our DNA. Our job is to help others to understand that all of these attributes are already within them. We just need to help them discover these things that they already have within and bring them to the surface. When they do, what power will be unleashed in their lives! When you help someone pull up that courage from deep within, you will see a change in them that will begin a change in the entire world! This change will ripple through nations and generations. Once you encourage someone, you teach them to encourage someone else. This begins a chain reaction stronger than any nuclear reaction in the universe!

Encourage yourselves daily while it is still "today."
Hebrews 3:13

Everyone is encouraged in different ways. Different people respond to different forms of encouragement. I have found that encouragement most often comes in three different forms: The Challenge, The Cheer and The Soft Touch. It is incumbent upon the Magnetic Christian to know these three different forms, or styles, of encouragement, and when to use them. Please understand that these three categories are very generalized. When and how to use each will always be influenced by many different factors – the person you are encouraging, their state of mind, the unique situation. Each of the three can be used in varying degrees. You will find yourself mixing and matching, sometimes using all three on the same person at the same time. It will always be up to you to figure out the subtle nuances of when to use each and to what degree. Before we discuss them, let me give you a word of encouragement. There will be times when you will fail. You will choose the wrong method, use the wrong words, perhaps even hurt someone's feelings. These things will happen. But don't ever let a temporary failure or setback stop you from continuing to be an encourager! As Winston Churchill told the British people at the depths of World War II, "Never, never, never give up!"

The Challenge

One of the favorite TV shows in my household is The Biggest Loser. On this show, very obese people are chosen to compete in a weight loss competition. Over the course of weeks and months, they shed copious amounts of weight. It is a very inspiring show. The trainers on the show are great examples of encouragement. If you watch the show, you'll see examples of all three forms of encouragement again and again. For many of the contestants, the most effective is The Challenge.

The Challenge is when you call someone out. You challenge them to achieve, to reach their full potential, to dig deep within and unearth the intestinal fortitude that God has given them. At the bottom line, The Challenge encourages someone to answer the following questions: How badly do you want it? What price are you willing to pay to get it? Are you ready to commit NOW to achieve that which you desire? Often The Challenge is done in an in-your-face way. Whether it concerns losing weight, giving up smoking, becoming a better husband and father, wife and mother, giving up a particular sin or anything else, sometimes we just need someone to drop the kid gloves, tell it like it is and challenge us to change.

I speak at many men's conferences. I have always found that men generally tend to respond well to The Challenge. This is not to say that women don't, but men tend to have a competitive streak in them and they want to rise to a challenge. This is why, at almost all of my talks to men's groups, I issue to them what I call "The 60-Second Challenge." I challenge men to pray with their wives for sixty seconds a day. Just one minute. And if they will commit to doing that for twenty-one days, chances are that it will become a habit – a habit that will transform their marriages and their lives. If you are a married person and you are not praying regularly with your spouse, I challenge you to try it beginning today.

I promise you it will bear fruit in your life. If you are not married but have a significant other, you should be praying with that person daily. Couple prayer is great glue for a relationship!

The Cheer

Go to pretty much any football game, from pee-wees to the pros and you'll see them on the sidelines, jumping up and down, shouting and always smiling – the cheerleaders. Have you ever thought about what the job of a cheerleader really is? It is to encourage! Cheerleaders are there to encourage the players and encourage the fans. If you notice, cheerleaders are encouragers to the bitter end. Even if their team is down 78-0, they still cheer on, encouraging everyone not to give up hope. You gotta love 'em!

Have you ever had a cheerleader in your life? Someone who has always been your biggest fan, celebrating every big and little achievement? For many people, that role was filled by their parents. This was certainly the case in my life. My mom and dad were there for every sporting event, every school play, every recital, everything. When I was in high school, I won a statewide pro-life speaking competition. When we got back to the small town where we lived, Mom and Dad took me to the local Holiday Inn where they had a congratulatory message put up on the large sign board by the busiest road in town. To this day I still have the picture of the three of us standing under that sign.

My wife and kids have also filled the role of cheerleader in my life. When I first started running marathons, Michelle and the kids were there at the finish line, shouting, clapping, screaming, making me feel like a hero. In our family, we have a tradition of breaking out the Red Plate whenever someone has a special achievement. It is just a big red plate that says, "You Are Special." I am very blessed, indeed.

At its core, The Cheer is simply positive reinforcement. This is often the most effective way to encourage people. Positive reinforcement works in most every area of life. When bosses and supervisors change from negative patterns to positive reinforcement, amazing things happen in the workplace. The same holds true in families, schools and even in the spiritual life. When you see someone doing good or doing well, give them The Cheer!

"Way to go!"

"Nice job!"

"You are awesome!"

"You can do it!"

"Keep it up!" (You'll notice that The Cheer is almost always ended with an exclamation point!)

I think it bears noting that so many people have never had a cheerleader in their lives. Perhaps this is the case for you. Many people never had parents that were supportive. They may never have experienced that teacher who really believed in them and encouraged them on to greater heights. For these folks, being an encourager can be a tough thing.

They never learned the fine art of positive reinforcement because they had so much negativity surrounding them in life.
If this is the case with you, I want to encourage you to stretch
yourself in this area. Always look for the good in others. Be
a cheerleader to someone you love. Believe in them, and let
them know you believe in them. I think you'll find that the
more you encourage others, the more you cheer others on,
the more courage you will find within yourself. Ask God to
help you be a cheerleader.

> *We urge you, brothers, admonish the idle,*
> *cheer the fainthearted,*
> *support the weak, be patient with all.*
> **1 Thessalonians 5:14**

The Soft Touch

We all go through tough times in life. It is part of our
human story. People we love die. Relationships break down.
We lose our job. Someone close to us is diagnosed with cancer or some other disease. These and so many other things
can be earth-shaking, life changing events. These are the
times that try men's souls. Often these trials and tribulations
are catalysts to questioning God, and sometimes even losing
faith in God. It's understandable enough, isn't it? And no one
is exempt. Take a look at St. Peter. Full of machismo and
bravado, Peter knew that he would never let Jesus down. Yet
when the going got tough, Peter got going. He denied Jesus
three times. And he wept bitterly because of his transgres-
sion.

Jesus knew that Peter needed encouragement to continue

in his ministry. Peter probably felt ashamed and disgusted with himself because he had denied even knowing Jesus. Because of Peter's potentially fragile state, Jesus knew that The Challenge and The Cheer were inappropriate forms of encouragement.

MAGNETIC INSIGHT:
Encouragement is about lifting others up. When our brothers and sisters get down – down on life, down on God, down on the future – we must be there to lift them up.

So Jesus chose The Soft Touch. After the resurrection, Jesus asked Peter three times if he loved Him. I feel pretty certain that Jesus' tone of voice was probably filled with empathy and love. (Can you imagine Jesus screaming like a drill sergeant, "DO YOU LOVE ME?!" Uh…I don't think so.)

The Soft Touch is used when people find themselves broken and vulnerable. While The Challenge may be attached with confidence and The Cheer associated with enthusiasm, The Soft Touch is most closely tied to compassion. The Magnetic Christian shares in the pain and sorrow of another and offers appropriate words of encouragement.

"Hang in there."

"This, too, shall pass."

"You can get through this."

"It's going to get better."

"I'm here for you."

Sometimes words just won't cut it. Perhaps you've heard of the famous saying attributed to St. Francis of Assisi: "Preach the gospel at all times; use words if necessary." I think that The Soft Touch is such a fitting name for this type of encouragement because often it does not include words at all; a simple touch will communicate more than words ever could. Have you ever just needed a hug? You didn't want someone to solve your problem or offer words of advice or spout platitudes. You just needed someone to hold you. These are the times when The Soft Touch works best.

Sometimes you may find that even a touch is not necessary. Many times our bodies, especially our faces, speak much more loudly than our voices ever could. I can recall more than a few times in my life when I was floundering, only to look out and see the face of my wife or my mom giving me a look of love and understanding that helped me get through. Think of the many different ways we communicate with our faces and our bodies. A smile, a wink or a nod can sometimes be all the encouragement someone needs to make it to the next step. A simple thumbs-up can give someone the energy to press on. Think of the many ways you can encourage someone without even a word or a touch.

Jesus as Our Example

Jesus is the model of encouragement. He told his disciples again and again that they would go through much hardship if they chose to follow Him. Yet He always encouraged perseverance. He let them know that, in the end, their reward would be great. He encouraged them never to quit, always to keep the end in mind. Perhaps His greatest words of encouragement came at the beginning of the Sermon on the Mount. They are the Beatitudes.

"Blessed are the poor in spirit,
for theirs is the kingdom of heaven.
Blessed are they who mourn,
for they will be comforted.
Blessed are the meek,
for they will inherit the land.
Blessed are they who hunger and thirst for righteousness,
for they will be satisfied.
Blessed are the merciful,
for they will be shown mercy.
Blessed are the clean of heart,
for they will see God.
Blessed are the peacemakers,
for they will be called children of God.
Blessed are they who are persecuted
for the sake of righteousness,
for theirs is the kingdom of heaven.
Blessed are you when they insult and persecute you and
utter every kind of evil against you [falsely] because of me.
Rejoice and be glad,
for your reward will be great in heaven."
Matthew 5:3-12

The culture today tells us it is okay to tear others down. Smack talk abounds, in sports and in life. Many people today are under the mistaken notion that by tearing others down, they somehow build themselves up. By gossiping, bullying, backbiting and making fun of others, we not only degrade others, we degrade ourselves. This kind of attitude and action is the antithesis of encouragement. Encouragement is about lifting others up. When our brothers and sisters get down – down on life, down on God, down on the future – we must be there to lift them up. Jesus spent his life encouraging people. The Scriptures are filled with encouragement. They help us to find that courage God has embedded into each and every one of us. As Magnetic Christians, can we do any less?

Blessed be the God and Father of our Lord Jesus Christ, the Father of compassion and God of all encouragement, who encourages us in our every affliction, so that we may be able to encourage those who are in any affliction with the encouragement with which we ourselves are encouraged by God. For as Christ's sufferings overflow to us, so through Christ does our encouragement also overflow. If we are afflicted, it is for your encouragement and salvation; if we are encouraged, it is for your encouragement, which enables you to endure the same sufferings that we suffer. Our hope for you is firm, for we know that as you share in the sufferings, you also share in the encouragement.
2 Corinthians 1:3-7

Questions for Reflection

1. Who have been models of encouragement for me in my life? How did they encourage me?

2. Am I a cheerleader for my spouse? My children? My family members? My workmates and classmates?

3. How can I be more encouraging to those closest to me? To those that I have difficulty with?

4. Do I spend more time tearing others down, or building them up?

5. Who are three people that I can encourage this week? How will I go about that?

Prayer

Father, forgive us for the times when we tear others down. Give us your spirit of encouragement, that we might lift others up, and encourage them to be the saints that you call us all to be. Give us new opportunities to be an encourager, and give us the courage to encourage all. Amen.

CONCLUSION

GO!!

"Go, therefore, and make disciples of all nations, baptizing
them in the name of the Father,
and of the Son, and of the holy Spirit, teaching them to
observe all that I have commanded you. And behold,
I am with you always, until the end of the age."
Matthew 28:19-20

Many years ago, we had a guy come to our home to give us an estimate on some work that needed to be done. Before he left, he asked if he could leave his business card with me. This wasn't your standard business card. In fact, the card did not have the name of the man's company on it at all. Here is what the card looked like:

John Smith
Disciple of Jesus Christ

If you would like to know more about
eternal life, call me at 555-1212
Matthew 28:19-20

Naturally, this led to much conversation. I asked him about his faith and we probably talked for 10 minutes or more about spiritual matters. One of the things I asked him was what kind of reaction he typically got when he handed people his card. As you might imagine, he got a very mixed bag of reactions from people. Most folks just smiled and said thank you. A few were downright hostile and offended. He shared that there were a small handful of people, though, who showed a genuine interest, and some who even took him up on his offer and called him. In his own way, this guy was truly following the mandate of Jesus in Matthew 28:19-20. (By the way, the name and phone number on the above card are not real. I honestly can't even remember his name.)

Would you be comfortable doing what that guy did? Would you find it easier to hand someone a business card than asking them point blank about whether or not they were interested in having a relationship with Christ? I think most folks would be uneasy with either of those two options. And that's fine. Here's the great thing about being an evangelist: the ways to share Christ with others are as numerous as the people that are called to do it. Everyone can come up with their own unique way of sharing their faith. We have discussed many ways, methods and forms of evangelization in this book. We must use all the tools at our disposal and tailor the message to each unique situation.

Follow This Rule

I want to share one thing that is a must for every situation. This iron clad rule is not only for evangelization opportunities, but for every facet of our lives. We need to follow this rule every minute of every day.

ALWAYS BE OPEN TO THE HOLY SPIRIT!

Jesus told his disciples as much.

"When they take you before synagogues and before rulers and authorities, do not worry about how or what your defense will be or about what you are to say. For the holy Spirit will teach you at that moment what you should say."
Luke 12:11-12

The same is true for us. It's fine to have an "elevator speech" prepared. Are you familiar with that term? It is something that is considered essential for business people. It is roughly a thirty to sixty second commercial for yourself. The term originated from people who found themselves on an elevator and were asked what they do. It is a great opportunity to make a new contact. You never know if a random meeting might turn out to be a long term relationship. So people began preparing a very short explanation of who they are and what they do. It works great in many situations. But for the work of evangelization, a cookie-cutter speech may not be the best way to go.

> **MAGNETIC INSIGHT:**
> *Have you ever said just the right thing at the right time? I have. I wish it would happen more often! When it does happen, you can be assured that it is the Spirit speaking through me.*

We must always be open to allowing the Spirit to speak through us. This raises a question, "How do we know if it is the Spirit speaking through us or just us speaking our mind?" It's a great question, and I wish I had a magical answer for it. But I don't. As with everything, there will invariably be times that we will fail. We will say the wrong thing. We may say something trite or even hurtful that will alienate another. When those times occur, we should try to rectify the situation, pray and learn from our mistakes.

On the other hand, there will be times when we are vessels of healing and encouragement. Have you ever said just the right thing at the right time? I have. I wish it would happen more often! When it does happen, you can be assured that it is the Spirit speaking through me. These are times when we must thank God for using us, for allowing us to be instruments of His peace. Can we make those times occur more frequently? You bet! How? By growing closer to God.

Have no anxiety at all, but in everything,
by prayer and petition, with thanksgiving,
make your requests known to God.
Then the peace of God that surpasses all understanding
will guard your hearts and minds in Christ Jesus.
Philippians 4:6-7

Practice, Practice, Practice

I have been exceptionally blessed to have many friends who are awesome Christians. These folks just ooze God's love. But this isn't something that just happened overnight.

Their godliness and loving nature has been nurtured through countless hours of getting to know Jesus. And the more they know Jesus, the more like Him they become; and the more like Jesus they become, the more magnetic they become! People want to be around them, they are drawn to them. I think every one of them would tell you that this doesn't come naturally. It takes plenty of work. The hard work of prayer, Scripture reading and meditating on God's word. I'm sure every one of them would say that the work is more than worth the effort.

Work. That word can be off-putting to many. I mean, don't we have enough work to do already? It's not like I need another job, another thing to add to my to-do list. We have to couch this in the proper context. This kind of work is the same kind of work we have to do in any relationship. Because, in the end, this is all about relationship. Just like I must work on my relationship with my bride, my children, my friends and my co-workers, so I must work on my relationship with God.

Is there a concrete way that we can get closer to God, which will in turn help us to become a more Magnetic Christian? Yes! It all starts with making a plan, setting goals.

GOAL!!!

I have always been a pretty goal oriented person. I have found that being a goal setter is helpful in every area of life. As I mentioned before, I am a runner. I have discovered through the years that if I do not have a goal, if I am not training for something specific, I lose focus very easily. You see, I have a propensity to be very lazy. When I don't have a goal, I have nothing to shoot for, nothing to train for. When that happens, it becomes very easy to not get out and run on any given day. Eh, I'll say, I don't have any races coming up, so I'll just blow off this one run. Unfortunately, one run becomes two, which becomes a week, which becomes a month that I haven't run. And if you have ever been on a regular program of anything, you know that you lose ability much faster than you gain it. It's not too long before I become very lazy and sedentary, and in a very short time I pretty much have to start over from scratch. This process works exactly the same in the spiritual life.

When I'm training for a race, I will set specific, small goals to help me reach my bigger goal. A typical week might look like this:

Monday: Cross train 1 hour
Tuesday: 5 miles of speed work
Wednesday: Cross train 1 hour
Thursday: Run 8 miles
Friday: Rest day
Saturday: Long run
Sunday: 5 mile recovery run

Each day I have a goal, and I have it written down. It is very important to write down goals. Because a goal not written down is just a dream. And dreams will get you nowhere if not acted upon. So, set one big specific goal, write it down and put a time limit on it. Then set smaller, specific goals that will help move you toward your bigger goal. If you've never tried this, start today. It will work wonders in every area of your life!

Do you not know that the runners in the stadium all run in the race, but only one wins the prize? Run so as to win.
Every athlete exercises discipline in every way.
They do it to win a perishable crown,
but we an imperishable one. Thus I do not run aimlessly;
I do not fight as if I were shadowboxing.
No, I drive my body and train it, for fear that, after having preached to others, I myself should be disqualified.
1 Corinthians 9:24-27

I bring up this practice of goal setting because this is very useful in enhancing our spiritual lives. If you desire to become a more Magnetic Christian, use this tool to help you along the way. Set a spiritual goal, then break it down into smaller goals. But remember, your goals must be very specific. For instance, say that your grand goal is this: To grow closer to Christ. That's fantastic! But it isn't very specific. Perhaps you could try something of a sub-goal – to spend more time in prayer and Scripture reading, or read the New Testament. Bravo! These practices will certainly help you toward your big goal of growing closer to Christ. Now, break it down into smaller goals that are specific. Make a plan that will move you closer to your bigger goal. Maybe your plan would look something like this:

Sunday: Get to church 15 minutes early to pray
Monday: Get up 15 minutes early and spend in quiet prayer
Tuesday: Read one chapter of a Gospel

Wednesday: Spend 15 minutes at lunch time reading the next chapter of the Gospel
Thursday: Take a 30 minute walk and pray for the intentions of others
Friday: Read two chapters of the Gospel
Saturday: Help a neighbor or do some sort of charity work

Now that looks like a plan! Small, manageable goals that will help you in your quest to achieving the bigger goal. Make your daily goals a priority. Don't let a day go by without achieving a goal. If you slip, if you get super busy and find that you didn't make your goal that day, don't beat yourself up. Just make sure you work on the goal the next day, because each day that you let it get away will make it that much harder to get back on track.

Your Life Verse

Scripture plays such an important role in our growth as Magnetic Christians. While being able to quote chapter and verse is nice, I don't think it is necessary. Quite honestly, I know that quoting chapter and verse to people can be somewhat off-putting.

> **MAGNETIC INSIGHT:**
> *We are called to love everyone. To love them enough to bring them to the only One who can fill the deepest desires of their soul.*

I'm not saying you should never do it, but, as we have discussed, tailor the message to the hearer. Many people are just not ready to be quoted chapter and verse to. I have found it much more effective to use phrases like, "Jesus said," or "St. Paul said," instead of "Well, the Bible says in First Corinthians eleven…" Many people may not even know you're quoting Scripture if you don't tell them. That can be just fine.

We must be immersed in Scripture to grow as Magnetic Christians. If a single word of Scripture never comes out of our mouths, it must be written in our hearts. The surest way to know God more is to read His story.

I would like to encourage you to do something that I think will be very helpful in your spiritual growth. Take a passage of Scripture and make it your own. Some people call this their "Life Verse." It can be anything at all, Old Testament or New Testament. Find a passage that speaks right into your heart and carry it with you always. Let it be a steady guide for you.

Here is my life verse:

The end of all things is at hand. Therefore, be serious and sober for prayers. Above all, let your love for one another be intense, because love covers a multitude of sins. Be hospitable to one another without complaining. As each one has received a gift, use it to serve one another as good stewards of God's varied grace. Whoever preaches, let it be with the words of God; whoever serves, let it be with the strength that God supplies, so that in all things God may be glorified through Jesus Christ, to whom belong glory and dominion forever and ever. Amen.
1 Peter 4:7-11

When you choose a life verse, remember that it doesn't have to be forever. As you grow in your walk with Christ, you may find another passage of Scripture that is more representative of where you are in that phase of your life. The key is to let God's word animate you and guide you into a deeper relationship with Him. Search through the Scriptures and find a passage that speaks directly into your heart, one that you can recall any time in any situation. Make them your words to live by. Write them down and keep them in your purse or your wallet or on your nightstand. Bring them to mind often. God's word will never let you down.

You Are Sent

After this the Lord appointed seventy[-two] others whom
he sent ahead of him in pairs to every town and place he
intended to visit. He said to them, "The harvest is abundant
but the laborers are few; so ask the master of the harvest to
send out laborers for his harvest. Go on your way; behold,
I am sending you like lambs among wolves."
Luke 10:1-3

When Jesus sent out the seventy-two, He told them to "ask the master of the harvest to send out laborers for his harvest." Could it be that Jesus was telling those people to pray for you? Hard to think of, since they lived nearly 2000 years ago. Yet I believe that is exactly what Jesus was saying. You see, just as Jesus sent out the Apostles and the seventy-two, so He sends you out to be a laborer in the harvest of souls. Yes, my friend, you are an apostle. The word apostle simply means "one who is sent." That means you and me. Jesus is sending us out into the world to bring souls to Him. How you decide to go about that mission is entirely up to you. You have been given all the tools, all the attributes necessary to be a Magnetic Christian. Now it is up to you to work on them and allow God to nurture them to their fullness.

Is this going to be an easy gig? Absolutely not. Just as He sent the seventy-two out "as lambs among wolves," so He sends us out. You will encounter much resistance. Satan will try to thwart you at every turn. Be prepared for that. But know that you are not alone.

Be sober and vigilant. Your opponent the devil is prowling around like a roaring lion looking for [someone] to devour. Resist him, steadfast in faith, knowing that your fellow believers throughout the world undergo the same suffer- ings. The God of all grace, who called you to his eternal glory through Christ [Jesus] will himself restore, confirm, strengthen, and establish you after you have suffered a little. To him be dominion forever. Amen.
1 Peter 5:8-11

In the end, this is all about love. As Magnetic Christians, we are called to love. Not just our family and friends and the people we go to church with. We are called to love ev- eryone. To love them enough to bring them to the only One who can fill the deepest desires of their soul. There are so many people in the world today, people near you, who are searching for love. They don't realize that they have a God- shaped hole in their hearts. Helping them find the Lover of their soul is a mission of the highest order. It is our mission. Call it evangelization, call it spreading the Gospel, call it anything you like. But most importantly, call it your life's work. I promise you it will be the most exciting adventure that you have ever undertaken. Now go out there and be a Magnetic Christian!

"I give you a new commandment: love one another.
As I have loved you, so you also should love one another.
This is how all will know that you are my disciples,
if you have love for one another."
John 13:34-35

Questions for Reflection

1. Am I comfortable talking about my faith? If not, why not?

2. Am I open to different forms of evangelization? What methods of sharing my faith have I had success with in the past?

3. Am I growing daily in my faith life? Do I have spiritual goals?

4. What concrete steps can I take in the next month to draw closer to God? Write down some spiritual goals.

5. Is there a particular passage of Scripture that has always stuck with me? What is it? Could this be my life verse? Set a goal to adopt a life verse soon.

Prayer

Father, I know that you have called me as a laborer in your field. Fill my heart with love for your people, that I may care for them enough to show them your love, and lead them to you. Amen.

ABOUT THE AUTHOR

Gus Lloyd and his wife, Michelle, have been married for over 31 years. They have four children, a greyhound and a cat. Gus began his radio career in 1979 and spent the next five years working at stations of nearly every format in Florida and Ohio. In 1984, Gus and his family moved to Tampa to start a family business. In the early 1990s, Gus returned to radio and hosted the popular morning show at Spirit FM in Tampa. In 2006, he was asked to host Seize the Day, the morning show on The Catholic Channel on Sirius XM Satellite radio. You can listen to Gus every weekday morning. He also writes a daily Scripture reflection on his web site, http://GusLloyd.com.

If you would like to order multiple copies of Magnetic Christianity for your small Christian community, Bible study or discussion group, contact Gus through his web site, http://GusLloyd.com.